PRAISE FOR

THE ART OF AMEN

"Seamlessly blending together sound biblical teaching, insightful personal testimonies, soul-stirring prayers, and beautiful drawings, *The Art of Amen* is truly a masterpiece! I cannot remember another book that touched my heart so deeply. Packed full of practical tips for building a stronger and more intimate prayer life, *The Art of Amen* is sure to leave your heart full and your prayer life transformed."

—**Jennifer Bleakley,** author of *Joey: How a Blind Rescue Horse Helped Others Learn to See*

"I love *The Art of Amen.* You are immediately drawn into Catherine's 'crafty' brilliance—no tired methods or stale prayer mechanics here! Her passion for praying the Word is real. This book is perfect for falling in love with Jesus all over again."

—**Rev. Dr. Jack Sheffield,** author of *God's Healing River* and *Genesis Seed*

"*The Art of Amen* is a beautiful tribute to the power of prayer. Catherine Bird's vulnerability in sharing her story invites you to rejoice in realizing that you are not alone in any feelings or insecurities you've ever had about talking with God. Thank you, Cat, for giving us all the tools we need to go on the prayer adventure of a lifetime!"

—**Erin Brown Hollis,** best-selling author of *Cheers to the Diaper Years* and *The Remarkable Housewives of the Bible*

"Maybe, like me, you grew up feeling there was just one way to pray. In *The Art of Amen*, Catherine Bird breaks that boxed-in thinking, showing us how to breathe new life and creativity into our conversations with God. Here we can find what we all long for: a relationship that is deep and intimate."

—**Lynn Cowell,** author of *Make Your Move* and *Brave Beauty*

"As a mental health professional, I have studied how spiritual practices like prayer lead to increased peacefulness and reduced anxiety. *The Art of Amen* leads readers through creative approaches to prayer with biblical examples, personal testimonies, and beautifully-designed artwork to inspire a deep calm in the midst of our hectic lives."

—**Michelle Nietert,** professional counselor and clinical director of Community Counseling Associates

I0809504

"Sometimes we hear the word *creative* and immediately feel inadequate. However, this book is an invitation for each and every one of us to embrace the reality of being made in the image of a creative God. Cat's grace and tenderness opens wide the doors to experience the joy of living a vibrant life as we worship a vibrant God!"

—**Teri Lynne Underwood,** author of *Praying for Girls*

"Jesus modeled discipleship, relationship, prayer, and so much more in the short time he lived on earth. Cat Bird pulls from his lessons and shows us how to pass them along to our children and incorporate them in every relationship. Gather your closest friends and dive deep into your prayer life with *The Art of Amen*."

—**Shontell Brewer,** author of *Missionary Mom*

"If you are looking for a book on prayer, you don't need to look any further than *The Art of Amen*! Catherine Bird has explored every type of prayer, from Genesis to Revelation. It is all here for us to read, digest, and be empowered to pray without fear. I highly recommend this book. Read and be blessed."

—**Rev. Dr. John K. Graham,** president and CEO of the Institute for Spirituality and Health

"Breaking through complacency and mundane life, *The Art of Amen* is a delightful glimpse into the creative side of prayer. It's perfect for the artsy creative and the craft-challenged alike."

—**Amy Elaine Martinez,** host of Real Victory Radio and author of *Becoming a Victory Girl*

"I'm a girl who thrives when biblical content is presented in a way that is fun and relatable. This is exactly what Catherine Bird has done with *The Art of Amen*. I know you'll enjoy it as much as I did!"

—**Courtney DeFeo,** author of *In This House, We Will Giggle* and founder of Treasured

"In *The Art of Amen*, Catherine chronicles her connection to prayer and to the God who listens and longs to be with us. It may be an art, it may be a rote ritual, but when you read this book, an 'amen' is sure to come."

—**Bob Mendelsohn,** director of AustralAsia, Jews for Jesus

"Prayer is an essential discipline for every Christian's faith walk, but it is also one that we often struggle with the most. Catherine's book is a great tool for building a great prayer life at any stage."

—**Kelly Stamps,** blogger at Kelly's Korner

THE ART OF Amen

A CREATIVE PRAYER EXPERIENCE

CATHERINE BIRD

LEAFWOOD
PUBLISHERS
an imprint of Abilene Christian University Press

THE ART OF AMEN
A Creative Prayer Experience

LEAFWOOD PUBLISHERS
an imprint of Abilene Christian University Press

ISBN 978-1-68426-220-5 | LCCN 2018052795

Printed in the United States of America

Published in Association with Jessica Kirkland and the literary agency of Kirkland Media Management, LLC. P.O. Box 1539, Liberty, Texas 77575.

Library of Congress Cataloging-in-Publication Data
Names: Bird, Catherine, 1976- author.
Title: The art of amen : a creative prayer experience / Catherine Bird.
Description: Abilene, Texas : Leafwood Publishers, 2019. | Includes bibliographical references.
Identifiers: LCCN 2018052795 | ISBN 9781684262205 (pbk.)
Subjects: LCSH: Prayer—Christianity.
Classification: LCC BV210.3 .B536 2019 | DDC 248.3/2--dc23
LC record available at https://lccn.loc.gov/2018052795

Cover design by ThinkPen Design | Interior text design by Sandy Armstrong, Strong Design

Interior illustrations and artwork by Shari Sasser

Leafwood Publishers is an imprint of Abilene Christian University Press
ACU Box 29138 | Abilene, Texas 79699

1-877-816-4455 | www.leafwoodpublishers.com

19 20 21 22 23 24 / 7 6 5 4 3 2 1

Contents

"May you look to those in heaven and continue their legacy of faith."

—SANDY FERGUSON

ACKNOWLEDGMENTS

This book was inspired by two incredible prayer warriors who I was blessed to call my mom and grandmother. While they are no longer on this earth, I find comfort knowing our faith binds us together and that we *will* be reunited one day.

Mama, I don't know how we're doing life without you, but somehow and in some way, God's sweet grace is enough. God is so good, too, because he often gifts us with tender reminders that the imprint of your life and love on this earth is still around us. Every soul you touched is gently reminded of how much you loved us when we see these God winks. These soft whispers of you fill our hearts, and we cling to them along with the knowledge that we will see you again. I miss you every single day. I love you.

Mama Gal, I imagine you sitting on a patio in heaven, rocking in your chair and smiling or laughing at someone or something. You taught us so many wonderful life lessons: how to make the best banana pudding ever; that your whole outfit can be thrown off if your hair doesn't feel right; and that there's no greater legacy than loving others well. I miss your face so much, and I look forward to the day when I can hear your "Hi, angel!" again.

Birthing a book is a process that takes a village, for sure. I thank God for the calling he has placed on my heart to share words of encouragement with each of you. This project would be nothing without him and the guidance of the Holy Spirit. The message within the pages of this book is near and dear to me, and it's such a joy to share it with you. I pray it blesses you.

I am also thankful for my Prince Charming, who is not perfect, but he *is* perfect for me. One of my favorite books is *Wuthering Heights* by Emily Brontë. There is a line in this book that beautifully conveys my love for the man God chose for me: "He's more myself than I am. Whatever our souls are made of, his and mine are the same." You're my rock, and I love you, honey.

Ashley and Emma Kathryn, you're my heart, girls. You two are such troopers during the busy writing seasons, and you just go with the flow. Mostly. This beautiful life God has given your daddy and me would not be the same without the two of you, and we are so blessed God entrusted you to us. I hope you always feel the security, not just of your parents' love, but of your heavenly Father's as well. You can never go wrong when you put your family first, and God should always be at the top of your list. Remember your legacy of faith, and stand firm in the truth of who you are and who God has called you to be.

Daddy, even though this book in a lot of ways is a love letter to Mama, it's also a love letter to you. I'm so thankful for the example of faith you and Mama set for Chris, Craig, and me. Our new normal without Mama looks different than anything we ever imagined for ourselves. And even though the last couple of years have been rocky and painful, we are still blessed, because we have one another. I love you.

The last two years have encompassed the toughest season I've ever endured. I would not have made it without my tribe, and more specifically the *Tribal Council*. You know who you are, and not a day goes by that I'm not thankful for each and every one of you. God used each of you to remind me that stormy seasons are fleeting, but the love of God and the gift of community are not. Your prayers and your love sustained me, and you'll never know just how much it meant to me when you knelt beside me in that broken place. #goldengirlsforever

My agent, Jessie, is a superhero, and her superpower is juggling about a thousand balls at once while never breaking a sweat. I have no idea how she accomplishes all she does in a day, but I am super thankful for her partnership. There's no fiercer advocate. You're good people, Jessica Kirkland.

FOREWORD

Less like a plea and more like a mandate, I screamed his name, "Jesus Christ! Help us!" I instinctually reached my arm across the chest of my then-twelve-year-old daughter, as if my feeble means would lessen the blow of the oncoming eighteen-wheeler, in my lane, traveling at sixty-plus miles per hour, headed straight for us. I swerved right; he swerved left. Then, in what seemed an eternity yet was simply an instant, my van, holding six-sevenths of everyone I dedicate my life to, found haven in a ditch off I-20 West near Tyler, Texas.

The baby never flinched. The sons chirped, "That was awesome!" and a daughter, I cannot recall which one, chastised, "Mother! You are not supposed to use the Lord's name in vain!" Dry-mouthed, shaken, and entirely thankful, I whimpered, "That was hardly in vain."

I hadn't thought of that dreadful scene much more until I sat down to compose this essay for my friend, Catherine Bird. Interesting, since it was a significant passage in a life played out in prayer, muddled in proper and flippant, answered and not.

Yes, I pray.

I would like to believe I am most steeped in the relational prayer that accompanies my walk with Jesus. I criticize my efforts. On days where I have overslept, missing my designated quiet time with him, I have come to recognize it doesn't lessen him, but it certainly hobbles me. Perhaps this is the greatest of tragedies in the Christian prayer journey: the belief that prayer is a mandate to activating the power of Yahweh. I have foolishly believed the God of all is less powerful, less invested, even careless if I do not follow through with my highfalutin plans to pray. It is for this reason I profess the belief that this book is so important, so timely, and so dear.

And it left me to wonder about my prayer life and its religiosity and craft, versus conversations with a Father who adored unto the death of his blameless Son. Certainly, I am grateful; still, I confess that running out of milk or a child with an ear infection can bring me to my knees. Also, I am easily distracted by shiny things, boy bands, and Lifetime Television murder mystery weekends.

He remains.

In my relationship with my husband, there are efforts to create time for dinner alone, outside our hectic schedules. There are organic conversations and methodical sit-downs. We may pass each other in the hall and reference a bill overdue or a reminder to pick a child up from the orthodontist. Then there are moments where we purposefully step back and reconcile what went wrong, and talk about how we can do better the next time. We plan romantic dinners alone, and when those impressive plans fall apart, we order takeout and watch reruns of *Seinfeld*.

At the core of my conversational relationship with my husband, there is room to create dialogue, embrace the organic, or simply get by for now. Within that dynamic, we are committed to each other and have carved out a life according to what it means to be Justin and Jami. Most certainly, as a lover of words married to man who embraces words few and far between, there have been some rough patches. But this is us. This is our groove, this is how we relate.

Furthermore, as I jotted notes about what I believe or used to believe about prayer, I took pause to think about the conversational relationship I have with the author of this beautiful book. Catherine, or *Cat* as her friends call her, has a sympathetic, darling voice. The first time I ever heard it, she left me a voice message, offering any help her family could lend my family after she learned of a hardship we were facing. It wasn't until several conversations later that I learned she had lost her precious mother merely weeks before she called to help me.

I love to talk to Cat. She is complimentary, sass, and kindness. She refers to her husband by his full name, which is hilarious and dear. "Travis Bird will be back later this evening." Or, "Travis Bird, Jami wants your fajita recipe." All this to say, I know her by our conversations. I grow in my understanding of her, and I delight in this friendship because we talk. And within those speeches we confess our devotion by laughing, crying, or simply chatting. Granted, if I never called her again, that would fade. However, the more we talk, the more I want to converse with her, and the more I understand her and her love of her God, her daughters, and the infamous Travis Bird.

In the pages of this book you will see beautiful artwork, timeless and important Scripture, and the craft of a wordsmith I am proud to call friend. However, I pray that you also uncover the unique thing that makes your prayers the cornerstone of your relationship with God. The things you say, the devotion, the rote, impersonal, desperate, formal, contrived, and passive words you direct at your heavenly Father are uniquely yours.

He knows you. He wants this ongoing dialogue with you unto his torturous death. The veil was torn, and nothing can stand between you and him. I fully believe you will be enriched by the pages that follow. It is all the things you want to say and the fun, simple, and imaginative ways to do it. It is the why and the how, it is scripturally sound, and it is all the things you may have missed in efforts to impress him. It is the adventure of creating a relational conversation with a God who calls you friend.

Prayer . . . it is complex and simple, profound and trivial, deep and shallow. It is a desperate plea for life and a flippant nod to moving the line at Starbucks. It is the carnal cry for healing and a muffled desire for last season's jeans to zip. It is intellect and folly, perfection and disaster, fury and thankfulness. It is confident and terrified. It is rote, memorized, and halfhearted. Next it is fragrant, genuine, and heartfelt. It is song, silence, passion, and complacency. It is moving and stagnant.

It is an adventure.

An art.

And no matter the acumen or nonsense, it is the very thing that brings you face-to-face with the living God. It is a privilege to introduce you to an author who prays well and loves better. Together, we invite you to the perfected mess in *The Art of Amen*. May you never pray the same.

—Jami Amerine,
author of *Stolen Jesus* and
Sacred Ground, Sticky Floors

PART ONE

Understanding Prayer

"IS PRAYER YOUR STEERING WHEEL OR YOUR SPARE TIRE?"

—CORRIE TEN BOOM

CHAPTER ONE

CREATED FOR COMMUNITY

We joined hands as a group, bowed our heads, and closed our eyes. Then I heard, "Would anyone else like to pray for us?" Dang it, Daddy. Pretty much everyone who knows my father knows he says crazy awesome prayers, and he also happens to be an ordained Episcopal priest. This explains the loud silence that followed his question.

I opened one eye and glanced around, noticing that everyone in the circle was studiously standing with head bowed and eyes closed, reminding me of what it's like to avoid the teacher's eyes at all costs, lest you be the one called on to speak in front of the class. Then it happened. My one open eye landed on my daddy's two open eyes, and they were staring right back at me.

Shoot. Busted. I was deer-in-the-headlights caught.

"Cat, would you like to pray for us?" he asked.

Thinking, "Not really," I responded with a bright, "Sure, but I'm not great at saying prayers aloud."

"That's OK; God doesn't mind," he said. "The priest doesn't have to be the one to always say the prayers. God likes to hear from all of us." Right.

Taking a deep breath, I went for it, feeling self-conscious and totally inept to be the person offering the prayer for our entire group. This wasn't just a family dinner. This was a large group of people, most of whom I did know, but a few I didn't (yet). We were in Israel taking in one of the many unforgettable places that were quickly turning my Bible into a pop-up book right before my eyes. Strangers milled about. I was acutely aware of my inadequacy to be praying aloud, but I forged ahead.

Of course, everyone was quite kind when the prayer was done, probably thankful they had dodged the praying-out-loud bullet themselves. Well, the good news was it would be a while before I was called on again, at least for that trip.

BUELLER? BUELLER?

One of my favorite movies from the 1980s is *Ferris Bueller's Day Off*. The storyline follows a fun-loving high school guy named Ferris Bueller, played by Matthew Broderick, who decides to feign illness in order to skip school and enjoy a day of relaxation instead. At the beginning of the movie, Matthew's character calls his best friend (Alan Ruck), who happens to actually be home sick, and talks his friend into joining him and Ferris's girlfriend for a day of fun.

While the boys are enjoying their day off from school, Ferris Bueller's sister must still go. We see a day of school through her eyes, and the audience is given a glimpse into the stereotypical day of a high school student. Hall passes were a thing, and so was detention. Popular kids and the not-so-popular kids often clashed. Some classes were more fun than others, and some classes even less so. This is where we are introduced to one of Ferris Bueller's most boring teachers. Ben Stein plays the role of Ferris Bueller's economics teacher. He's super dry and calls roll by the students' last names. For me, it was a really memorable part of the movie to hear Ben Stein saying in his droll voice, "Bueller? Bueller?"

Often this scene comes to mind when I am in a group where a volunteer is asked to pray. Usually, silence ensues. Then I want to call out, "Bueller? Bueller?" Actually, I sometimes do. For those who are familiar with this cult classic, it always brings a chuckle.

Seriously, though. Why are we so hesitant to pray?

WHAT IS PRAYER?

Merriam-Webster defines prayer as "an address (such as a petition) to God or a god in word or thought," "a set order of words used in praying," and "an earnest request or wish." I love this definition, but for me, prayer is simply an open, honest conversation with God. The truth is, we all bear the image of a loving God (Gen. 1:27), are crafted for a specific purpose (Eph. 2:10), and were designed to delight in community (Gen. 1:26)—not just with our creator—but with one another as well (Rom. 12:10). So it makes sense that we long to feel connected. God did that on purpose.

Our God is also deeply creative. We have only to glimpse the world around us to see plainly how imaginative our creator is. A multitude of colors paint the various landscapes where we live, and they are vast and varied. Goodness, the human body is even a marvelous wonder, how so many tiny parts and pieces work together. The birds of the skies, the fish of the sea, and the animals of the land all reflect the artistic nature of God.

So why can't prayer be both relational and creative? I believe it can be both, and that is the heart behind this book. I really want to unpack the why and how of prayer and lead readers through a deeper exploration of creative ways we can pray beyond a regular quiet time.

I've wanted to write this book for a long time. For years, I have listened to moms and their kids in Bible study class after Bible study class struggle with the act of prayer, and not just praying aloud. As I began to really pay attention, I noticed many of us—small and tall (how I refer to children and adults)—are self-conscious about the words we offer to God through prayer. If these are supposed to be our petitions and earnest requests to God, why are we so hesitant to share them with the One who created us? He already knows our hearts, but he wants us to share with him. As a mom, I can often read the mood of my children, but I want to hear from their lips how they are feeling and why they are feeling the way they are.

I think my own insecurities about prayer actually stem from growing up with liturgical prayer. Hear me out, friends. I love liturgical prayers. They are beautiful. There is comfort to be found in recitation of confessional prayer, the Apostles' Creed, the Nicene Creed, and the many other prayers I've learned from the *1979 Book of Common Prayer* over the years. The challenge for me is that these prayers are so wonderful that I've often felt like my words don't measure up to the beauty conveyed in these pre-written offerings. Or Ann Voskamp. Oh, my goodness. Talk about a lyrical linguist.

It has taken me years to find comfort in the truth that *my* words *and yours* are just as beautiful to God as the authors' words in the *Book of Common Prayer.* Not only are our words beautiful to God, but our prayers to him also serve as an act of worship. Take a moment to read the following two verses and write them in the space below:

Philippians 4:6

1 Thessalonians 5:16–18

The Bible says we are to pray and remain thankful, then repeat. Think about the impact of prayer when we come before God with a humble heart of hope, expectation, and thankfulness. God isn't looking for the perfect soliloquy. He is well aware he hasn't created each of us with the gift of poetry and song. Although I often joke that when I'm in the shower or my car, I sing *just* like Celine Dion, or if I'm really feeling sassy, Pink. And when I pray alone, I sound *just* like Ann Voskamp. True story. Well, the truth is I may not be gifted with the ability to belt out a song, but my words do sound like music to God's ears. When we open our hearts and mouths to communicate with our Lord, it serves as an awesome act of worship.

Personally, I sometimes overcomplicate what is really rather simple. I'm sure this never happens to *you*, or maybe you can relate. The Martha in me once thought prayer required the perfect quiet place, the perfect words to offer, and the perfect trust that God will hear and answer my prayers (and just maybe in the timeframe I kindly suggest).

I love being a wife and mom, friends. I do. However, my sweet baby girl who just entered her teen years did not sleep through the night until she was nearly three-and-a-half years old. I learned as a young mom why sleep deprivation is a real form of torture. There were days when I simply held my Bible in my hands, because I was too tired to open it and read. A very wise mentor shared with me a tidbit about prayer during that time that I've never forgotten. She told me in those seasons—where quiet space is at a premium, words are at a loss, and God remains silent—to find opportunities to pray and worship in the crazy rhythm-of-rush season where I am.

I learned to listen to my baby's laugh and give thanks to God for entrusting me with such a precious, sleepless little thing. I delighted in the warm embrace of my husband at the end of a long day, giving thanks that he didn't seem to mind when my hair wasn't brushed and my pants were inside out *and* backwards (yes, this really happened and, sadly, more than once). I relished encouraging words offered by friends who continued to love me unconditionally through difficult seasons.

AN OPEN, HONEST CONVERSATION

My friend Bobbie and I were talking the other day. She and I were visiting about this book—more specifically this chapter. We frequently keep in touch by phone, by text, and by an introvert's dream-of-an-app called Marco Polo. We often visit about mundane things, but we also share the depth of what's in our hearts—what may be lifting them up or weighing them down. Nothing is too trivial or too big. Any topic is fair game. Our relationship is easy, comfortable, and yet unbreakable. Our hearts have been knit together, and we embrace all that means.

Now, if I were to stop calling, texting, or communicating with Bobbie, her love for me wouldn't die. However, our relationship would likely change, and it is also likely we would cease being as close we are without regular and honest connection.

This is how I've come to view prayer with God.

A STROLL THROUGH THE GARDEN

The first time prayer is mentioned in the Bible is Genesis 4:26, which says, "Seth also had a son, and he named him Enosh. At that time people began to call on the name of the LORD" (NIV).

However, if we define prayer as an easy, open, honest conversation with God, then the first prayers were actually between Adam and Eve with God in the Garden of Eden. Can you imagine? Perfect beauty. The Garden of Eden. Adam and Eve were created for community with God. He delighted in his creation of them. He spent time with them. He listened. They talked. He talked. They listened.

Yes, sin entered the world, and Adam and Eve were cast out of the Garden of Eden. Yet God did not abandon them. On the flip side, though, God also did not promise them their lives would be easy and free of trials. We know from Scripture that they worked hard by the sweat of their brows (Gen. 3:19). One of their children would grow up to slay another sibling (Gen. 4:8). The heartache and trials had to be grueling. Yet God was still present. Scripture literally begins and ends with the presence of God. First:

> In the beginning God created the heavens and the earth. Now the earth was formless and empty, darkness was over the surface of the deep, and the Spirit of God was hovering over the waters. (Gen. 1:1–2 NIV)

The Garden of Eden may have been Adam and Eve's first home, but it was sacred because it was also where God physically communed with them (Gen. 3:8).

Flip to the end of your Bible, and witness the same image on a much grander scale, when all of heaven has collided with the whole earth to make a perfect sanctuary for God to dwell with man:

> Then I saw a new heaven and a new earth, for the first heaven and the first earth had passed away, and the sea was no more. And I saw the holy city, new Jerusalem, coming down out of heaven from God, prepared as a bride adorned for her husband. And I heard a loud voice from the throne saying, "Behold, the dwelling place of God is with man. He will dwell with them, and they will be his people, and God himself will be with them as their God. He will wipe away every tear from their eyes, and death shall be no more, neither shall there be mourning, nor

> crying, nor pain anymore, for the former things have passed away." (Rev. 21:1–4 ESV)

In the book of Revelation, Eden returns and has expanded into a new heaven and a new earth where all of God's people enjoy his presence eternally. Talk about "And they lived happily ever after!"

But we are living in the middle of the story. Trials and hardships are a guarantee during our lives on earth. God did not promise we wouldn't endure such experiences, but he did promise we wouldn't do so alone. Prayer is our lifeline to our creator, a loving God, who longs for us to share with him in an easy, open, honest relationship.

EMBRACING COMMUNITY AROUND US

As an introvert, I tend to recharge my batteries by spending time alone, preferably in nature. I love to sit on my patio and hear the birds sing, the squirrels chatter, and the leaves rustling in the wind. Oh, these things make my heart so happy.

It is not uncommon for me to withdraw from my friends and community from time to time and slip down into what we now all refer to as "Cat's hidey-hole." When I'm "in the hole," so to speak, I rarely pop on social media, talk on the phone, or attend larger events. I skip these things in favor of hot yoga class, long walks in nature, and nesting at home. My husband especially loves these times (he's rolling his eyes right now), because it's often when I focus on home projects and feel inspired to tackle Pinterest inspirations (which inevitably require his help). I also escape into my hidey space when I'm writing or pressed to meet a deadline, but I have been known to sneak away just for the sake of silence and solitude.

Now, having said all that, I am blessed with an awesome tribe. I prayed for a word to meditate on and embrace at the beginning of 2017, and I laughed when God answered my prayer with a most unexpected word. My mom had been diagnosed with cancer the September before, and it had already been a roller coaster of a few months. What I thought I needed was rest. Yet the word God pressed upon my heart was *community*.

That next twelve months was the toughest season I've ever endured. I would not have survived it without my community. God knew I wasn't supposed to go through that experience alone. Friends took children to school, sometimes keeping them overnight so I could be with my mom and dad in Houston. Friends brought meals, because my children insist on eating every day. Friends sat in silence with me when I was completely out of words and cried with me when I was full of nothing but tears.

I'll share more about my mom a little further into the book, and you'll see her words of wisdom peppered throughout the chapters. She was a fierce prayer warrior and lent many words of wisdom to those around her. Prayer was one of my mom's favorite things to do, and as she was such an encourager, I want to share her encouragement with you. (Look for the "Sandy says" pullout boxes for an extra-special note or prayer on the topic we're discussing.)

The point is that God blessed me with community, a rock-solid tribe, who stood strong when all I could do was kneel in my brokenness. Your community is that same gift from God to you. Scripture is rich with instruction about how we are to love one another. A few of these passages follow.

> A new commandment I give to you, that you love one another: just as I have loved you, you also are to love one another. By this all people will know that you are my disciples, if you have love for one another. (John 13:34–35 ESV)

> Finally, brothers, rejoice. Aim for restoration, comfort one another, agree with one another, live in peace; and the God of love and peace will be with you. (2 Cor. 13:11 ESV)

> For you have been called to live in freedom, my brothers and sisters. But don't use your freedom to satisfy your sinful nature. Instead, use your freedom to serve one another in love. (Gal. 5:13)

> Be kind and compassionate to one another, forgiving each other, just as in Christ God forgave you. (Eph. 4:32 NIV)

> Everything in the world is about to be wrapped up, so take nothing for granted. Stay wide-awake in prayer. Most of all, love each other as if your life depended on it. Love makes up

> for practically anything. Be quick to give a meal to the hungry, a bed to the homeless—cheerfully. Be generous with the different things God gave you, passing them around so all get in on it: if words, let it be God's words; if help, let it be God's hearty help. That way, God's bright presence will be evident in everything through Jesus, and *he'll* get all the credit as the One mighty in everything—encores to the end of time. Oh, yes! (1 Pet. 4:7–11 MSG)

At the very center of community is the God who created it. Our God, the creator of all things (Col. 1:16), in his perfect wisdom, crafted us to crave what we need most aside from him—and that is one another.

Sandy Says

"Is God good or what?"

A BEAUTIFUL BLEND OF PRAYER AND COMMUNITY

by Bobbie Schae

I did not grow up *in the faith*, so I was an adult when I asked Jesus into my heart. I wasn't exactly sure what *faith* was supposed to look like. As a new Christian, one of the first prayers I found myself continually repeating was, "Lord, bring me a friend to walk with on this new path." You see, when Jesus saved me, it wasn't a subtle change. It was more like a renovation. Jesus didn't just come in and tidy up the place and apply a fresh coat of paint to the walls in my heart. I was a complete and total overhaul. I was stripped down to the studs and utterly remade.

Everything seemed to change at once, and this was OK. I found myself willingly laying aside much of the old me in order to give this new me an opportunity to come forth. My heart and my desires changed, which ultimately meant that my lifestyle was reformed as well. My relationships and my community were also altered, because I no longer went to the same places or engaged in the same things that I had done before Jesus transformed me.

I was like one of the homes on *Fixer Upper*! I loved the remodeling that had taken place in my spirit, but I had so many questions and thoughts. I was craving community. I needed a real, authentic, rich friendship where I could connect heart-to-heart with another sister in Christ. I longed for someone to journey with me who really understood and who could be an encouragement to me in this season.

I began to pray that God would bring a friend, another believer, into my life. This became a prayer that I prayed often and one that God has been beyond faithful and generous in answering over the years. That first year, he sent a couple that came alongside my husband and me and acted not only as friends, but as mentors in the very early years of our salvation. Later, in a difficult season of life, he sent a more seasoned woman into my life to help me grow as a wife and a young mom.

Shortly after that, God gifted me with an entire community of Christian girlfriends as he opened the door for me to be part of a variety of new ministries. As I continued to step in faith, God anticipated each step, providing the community support he knew I would need. The journey has taken a few years, but God has provided a way for me to be deeply connected with quite a few women who build me up and encourage me in my faith walk while I am able to do the same for them. It's a beautiful manifestation of how God calls us to love one another.

Honestly, I almost feel a little guilty telling you about the over-the-top generous way in which God has answered this prayer in my life. Take my sweet friend Cat, who is writing this beautiful book for you. She is a precious gift from a loving Father. She is an answer to that prayer I prayed all those years ago. We've spent countless hours talking, praying, encouraging one another, and sharing truth and God's Word with one another. She exemplifies the type of friend that I prayed for, and she makes me a better person and a better Jesus follower.

But here's the thing, friend. God knows we *all* need and crave community where we can love one another as our authentic selves, and he designed us this way on purpose. There is something unbelievably beautiful that happens when women come together in the name of Jesus for the purpose of linking arms, loving each other well, and living in community together.

Trust me, I know. It isn't always easy. Sometimes it is downright scary! But, hear me, sweet friend. It is all worth it. God created us for community. He does not intend for us to walk alone. He knows that we are better together. If you have that kind of community surrounding you, you are one blessed gal. Say a prayer of thanksgiving for that gift. If not, below is a prayer just for you similar to the one that I prayed so fervently for myself all those years ago.

> Father God,
>
> We love you. You are a good and generous Father who gives abundant gifts to his children. Father, you did not create us to walk through this life alone. You created us to belong to a rich and deep community. You created us to be part of a body of believers.
>
> Heavenly Father, I pray that even now, you would begin to knit the heart of this dear reader to another believer. I pray for a friend to join her in the journey. Lord, I pray for someone whom she can be vulnerable with, whom she can let her guard down with, and whom she can be entirely herself with. I pray for a friend who will sharpen

her as iron sharpens iron, but also one who will be gentle with her heart and love her well.

I pray that you will bring this dear reader someone who will build her up and encourage her in her faith walk. I ask that the friend you send will draw her closer to you.

Lord, equip this sweet reader to be that kind of friend, as well. Give her a heart to love and encourage. Create in her the desire to spur someone else along and to hold the hand of a dear sister who is also on this journey of walking wherever you lead.

Father God, we trust you. We know that you already have someone in mind. We know that you are already at work orchestrating their meeting, turning their hearts toward one another, and creating the opportunities for them to truly connect. We place this need in your hand, God, and we believe that you will answer it in a way that far exceeds our expectations.

We love you, Lord. Thank you for the gift of community. Thank you for sisterhood and friendship. Thank you for the unity that comes through you.

In Jesus's holy name we pray,

Amen

CHAPTER TWO

Why Do We Pray?

We know what prayer is, but why do we pray? The why behind prayer is really simple. When we pray, our relationship with God grows. Remember my friend Bobbie and how she and I regularly communicate as we share both mundane and mammoth things happening in our daily lives? A healthy relationship consists of regular communication, which involves speaking and listening.

I adore author and speaker Priscilla Shirer. I listen when she speaks and have heard her do so on many occasions. However, her talking and my listening does not constitute a relationship (as much as I may wish that were so). She doesn't know me, and though I would like to, I don't really know her. A relationship between Priscilla and I would require effort and time from both of us, not a one-sided perspective where only she speaks and I listen.

Healthy relationships require speaking *and* listening from both parties. If we agree that this is true, then it makes sense that prayer is relational and includes both speaking and listening between God and ourselves. While fellowship with God is the goal, we may not always start out that way. Think about some of your early prayers. What did they look like?

Perhaps you first cried out to God in a time of need.

"Help me, Lord!"

"Lord, I need you!"

"Lord, can you provide . . . ?"

"Lord, I'm lost."

In a way, our early prayer life is quite childlike, but think about this for a second. Children do not just turn to their parents for wants and desires. How often do children climb in their parents' laps simply to be held? Friends, my seventeen-year-old daughter *still* crawls into my lap nightly just for a hug. I am not complaining, either, because I love that this is part of our regular routine.

As a parent, I cherish those moments when my children just want to sit and cuddle. My younger daughter slept with a small, soft lovey from the time she was a baby until she decided it was time to be a "big girl" and sleep without him. His name was Purple Lovey. Probably not surprisingly, he was lavender. His cute little bunny head held a rattle inside, and from his neck flowed the soft blanket of his body. I knew the instant Emma Kathryn awoke from her naps when she was younger, because I could hear Purple Lovey begin to rattle.

Often I used her naptimes to focus on consultant work, but the minute I heard Purple Lovey, I would stop, turn in my desk chair, and wait for my little girl to round the corner. Oh, my heart. The sleepy face of my precious little girl melted me every single time. I relished those long minutes when she would crawl in my lap after her nap just to be held and loved. If this is how we feel as parents, and we are the image bearers of God, how much greater is his love for us? It is unfathomable, friends.

So perhaps your early prayers reflect a childlike quality, but that's not a negative thing at all. Jesus said, "Let the little children come to me and do not hinder them, for to such belongs the kingdom of heaven" (Matt. 19:14 ESV). While prayer surely encompasses our heartfelt desires and requests, our heavenly Father longs for us to crawl into his lap just for the sake of snuggles, too. Have you ever just sat in silence asking the Holy Spirit to wash over you? Sometimes we need to sit and whisper, "I love you, Abba Father. Will you hold me?"

WHAT A FRIEND WE HAVE IN JESUS

My best gal pal in the world and I are about to celebrate our twentieth anniversary of friendship. Neither of us had any idea when I walked into her office in the College of Architecture at Texas A&M University all those years ago what a gift God was giving us. We have walked through a lot of life together. Job opportunities, job loss, the births of all of our babies, moves, death of loved ones, the devastating illness of my mom . . . the list goes on and on.

All of those big life experiences are sandwiched between everyday moments sometimes full of laughs, sometimes full of tears, and containing no small number of Sonic happy hour runs. When I have fun news to share, she is one of the first people I call. In those tough moments when life has taken me to my knees, she is one of the first people to kneel next to me. Friendships like ours are rare and precious, and we recognize it for the blessing it is.

This is the kind of relationship Jesus wants with each and every one of us. When we have fun news to share, he wants to be the first name we think to call. In those tough moments when life takes us to our knees, he is ever-present and kneeling next to us. Friendship with Jesus is precious, an incredible blessing that is available to each and every one of us.

One of my favorite hymns is "What a Friend We Have in Jesus." Take just a moment and look up the lyrics. Write them in the space below.

"What a Friend We Have in Jesus"

by Joseph Scriven and Charles Converse

Look at these words again.

> What a privilege to carry
> Everything to God in prayer!
> O what peace we often forfeit,
> O what needless pain we bear,
> All because we do not carry
> Everything to God in prayer!

When my BFF and I share one another's burdens, it lightens our load considerably. How often do you feel better after talking through what is weighing down your heart, or when you're finally able to share the fun news that was about to burst inside of you? Jesus longs to be that kind of friend to us. He paid the blood price so that we may have this beautiful relationship with him, and the gift is ours to accept. All we have to do is reach for his hand.

We pray because we want a deeper relationship with God.

LEARNING FROM THE MASTER

The best example we have for prayer was modeled by Jesus himself (Matt. 26:36; Mark 1:35; Luke 6:12). In Chapter Five, we'll unpack the framework of prayer and the words Jesus taught us to pray (Luke 11:1–4). For now, it's important to note that Jesus himself prayed and prayed often (Luke 5:16).

If prayer is fellowship with God, it shouldn't surprise us that Jesus prayed. Jesus prayed as the Son of God to God the Father. As the eternal Son of God, Jesus prayed out of his divinity as the Son of God—serving as a display of communion with his Father (John 1:18; John 10:30). Yet he prayed out of his humanity as well—serving as a model for us of what dependence on our heavenly Father looks like. Jesus regularly demonstrated why and how we can earnestly turn to our good, good Father in heaven for our thanksgivings and petitions. We need only turn to Scripture for evidence of how Jesus prayed.

Jesus prayed *with other people*. Luke 9:28 tells us that Jesus took some of his disciples up a mountain with him to pray. Jesus praying with his disciples demonstrates the importance of praying together, which Acts 1:14 also emphasizes: "They all met together and were constantly united in prayer, along with Mary the mother of Jesus, several other women, and the brothers of Jesus." While we don't know for sure whether Jesus was present at the time of this particular convergence, Scripture is clear that Christians gathered together to pray (Acts 2:42).

Jesus prayed *for others*. Scripture shares examples of Jesus's intercessory prayers, which is what we call prayers for other people (Luke 22:32; John 17). We will dig deeper into this type of prayer and creative ways to explore it in Chapter Eight, but look at the example in Luke 22:32 as Jesus explains how he interceded on behalf of Simon: "But I have pleaded in prayer for you, Simon, that your faith should not fail. So when you have repented and turned to me again, strengthen your brothers" (Luke 22:32).

Jesus prayed *alone*. I love that while Jesus taught us the value of praying together (Matt. 18:20), he also modeled the importance of praying alone (Matt. 26:36). I relish the thought that Jesus often withdrew into nature to pray. In this crazy rhythm-of-rush pace that so many of us keep, distractions abound. There is something so simple and elemental about withdrawing to a quiet place where we can pray while simultaneously taking in God's handiwork (Ps. 19:1). "But Jesus often withdrew to the wilderness for prayer" (Luke 5:16).

Scripture makes it clear that prayer was very important to Jesus. He demonstrated to us that prayer is *purposeful* and *effective*. The Bible tells us Jesus rose early in the morning, sometimes went without sleep, and withdrew in solitude—all for the sake of prayer. Through prayer, he made decisions, performed miracles, and overcame difficult situations. In contrast, we often pray *when we have time*. Jesus showed us prayer was an integral and seamless part of his human life. His prayer reflected his personal relationship with God, and he trusted in God's will regardless of the outcome of his earnest requests.

Because we aren't Jesus, we will certainly fall short of the model of prayer he gave us. But you know what? God doesn't expect you to be anyone or anything other than the authentic person he created you to be, and that is the person with whom he longs to have a relationship. Some of the most complicated of feelings can often explained with the simplest of words. My mind drifts back to how elementary my prayers sometimes feel when compared to others who I think are much better at praying than I am. Yet, the truth is God created me as I am, with purpose—just as he has done with each of you. Only I can share my heart with God because there is only one me. Only you can share the depths of your heart with God because there is only one you. In the words of the wise Dr. Seuss, "Today you are You, that is truer than true. There is no one alive who is Youer than You."[1] Isn't that the truth?

BIBLICAL MENTORS

We find plenty of other examples of praying men and women throughout the Bible, people who teach us to pray consistently and boldly. Let's take a peek at just a few of my favorites.

KING JEHOSHAPHAT

King Jehoshaphat was the fourth king of Judah, and we are first introduced to him in 1 Kings 22:42. By the time we reach 2 Chronicles, we learn the armies of the Moabites, Ammonites, and some of the Meunites have declared war on Jehoshaphat. Oh, boy.

Wisely, Jehoshaphat prays to the Lord and asks for help to defeat what look like pretty unfavorable odds. Jehoshaphat tells his people that the Lord says, "Do not be afraid! Don't be discouraged by this mighty army, for the battle is not yours, but God's" (2 Chron. 20:15). Jehoshaphat then puts singers (*singers*, y'all) in front of his battle-ready soldiers, ordering them to sing praises to Jehovah as they march toward battle.

As Jehoshaphat's people near the battle, God causes the enemy soldiers to fight among themselves. When the Israelites arrive, every enemy soldier is dead! This put (literally) the fear of God into Jehoshaphat's enemies, so that there was peace in the land (2 Chron. 20:29–30). Jehoshaphat sought God's guidance continually through prayer and trusted God to protect him and his people.

THE PROPHET ELIJAH

Elijah was an Old Testament prophet who shows us through Scripture what it means to be bold with our prayers. He prayed with incredible faith, believing that God was able to answer even the most audacious of prayers. For example, James 5:17–18 reads, "Elijah was as human as we are, and yet when he prayed earnestly that no rain would fall, none fell for three and a half years! Then, when he prayed again, the sky sent down rain and the earth began to yield its crops."

While we may not be able to relate directly to a drought of rain and the resulting impact of what that means for a successful harvest, many of us understand figuratively that a drought means a period of going without.

I live in Texas where we actually do have extended periods of triple-digit heat and rainless days. We've been on watering restrictions for several years. However, there are droughts of other kinds, too. When I asked my husband and kids for examples of what they would consider a figurative drought, I was thinking they would share a heartfelt story about a spiritual drought and so on. Instead, this is what I heard.

Kids: "Remember when we were in the Grand Tetons and Yellowstone, and we didn't have cell service for almost two weeks? That was a drought." #firstworldproblemsforsure

Husband: "Sports, babe. The Aggies haven't beat the LSU Tigers in seven years."

Elijah might be shaking his head, but his lesson isn't lost on us. Come boldly and lay your most audacious prayers at God's feet, and whether it's to bring rain or a much-longed-for win against your biggest football rival, God receives them all.

THE PROPHETESS ANNA

Anna was a New Testament prophetess who recognized the infant Jesus as the awaited Messiah (Luke 2:36–28). We know from the Gospel of Luke that Anna was both married and widowed at a very young age, but by the time we meet her in Scripture, she is an old woman of eighty-four years. We also know from Luke's testimony that Anna never left the temple, and she prayed without ceasing.

Here's what I love about the short story of Anna. God's people had not yet received the Holy Spirit, so the temple was an outward symbol of the presence of God. Being a woman *and* a widow, Anna was likely not wealthy, nor did she likely hold an important social status. She could have been easily overlooked and forgotten. Yet instead of wallowing in the very sad circumstances of her early widowhood, Anna pursued the presence of God without ceasing. This meant that she remained at the temple for decades, long before Mary and Joseph visited with baby Jesus. She could have embraced bitterness, but instead she emoted faith. She embraced what Scripture tells us, which is to pray and remain thankful.

Some of my sisters reading these words right now are facing very sad circumstances, and perhaps the future looks bleak and unsure. Well, here's what you can be sure of. When Jesus was crucified, the veil was torn, and our God who created the heavens and earth will never again dwell in a temple made with hands (Acts 17:24). Jesus, through his death, removed the barriers between God and man, and now we may approach our Lord with confidence and boldness (Heb. 4:14–16).

He sees you, friend. He crafted you with love and purpose, and the God who knows the number of hairs on your head will not forsake you (Luke 12:7). The enemy would have you embrace bitterness and defeat, but we know the truth. The enemy has already been defeated, and you are free to pursue God relentlessly and fearlessly. Just like Anna, you are the daughter of a king.

MODERN-DAY PRAYER WARRIORS

While the Bible is full of men and women who beautifully model prayer for us, there are plenty of modern-day prayer warriors who continue to reflect the power of prayer. We can also glean helpful practices from these inspiring people and apply them to our own prayer lives.

One caveat, because Travis Bird says I need to tell you that when I say "modern-day prayer warriors," I'm referring to folks who have lived more recently (like, say, the last three hundred years or so). I know it's not Marvel Avengers modern, but it is *totally* modern if you're taking into consideration the people of the ancient world, right? Right.

OK, so here we go.

GEORGE MÜLLER

George Müller (1805–1898) is widely considered one the greatest men of prayer and faith since the days of the New Testament. He is probably best known for his orphanages, through which he provided thousands of children with food, clothes, and education.

He also kept prayer journals. In George Müller's journals, he recorded more than *fifty thousand* experiences with answered prayer, thirty thousand of which he said were answered the same day or the same hour that he prayed them. Take a minute and ponder this. That's roughly eight hundred answered prayers each year, more than once per day for more than sixty years.

OK, so I know most of us in our rhythm-of-rush lives don't have time to record all of our prayers, but George Müller was on to something. He also was open about his struggle to concentrate during his prayer time, saying he easily lost focus due to the distractions around him. The man recorded more than fifty thousand answered prayers, and he was surrounded by hundreds of children every single day. Suddenly, my busy schedule with two rambunctious teenagers doesn't sound like such a solid excuse.

It's OK, friends. There is neither shame nor judgment here. Admittedly, George Müller didn't have to answer a hundred daily emails, hear the constant ping of his cell phone, or deal with the same kinds of distractions that we face today. However, he still struggled with them, and he left for us an incredible record of God's faithfulness through prayer. That's what we can take away from George Müller's example of prayer.

JOHN WESLEY

In the movie *War Room*, my friend Priscilla Shirer gave a lovely performance in her role as Elizabeth Jordan. Elizabeth and her husband are struggling in their marriage, but with the help of a new friend, Miss Clara (Karen Abercrombie), Elizabeth learns the transformative power of prayer. Elizabeth turns her bedroom closet into a prayer room, or as Miss Clara calls it, her war room.

My mom loved this movie and couldn't wait to turn the nook in her upstairs space into her very own prayer war room, which she used daily for as long as she could climb the stairs. Undoubtedly, *War Room* inspired many of us to set up our own prayer spaces.

Well, before the *War Room* and my good friend Priscilla, there was John Wesley and his prayer closet. John Wesley (1703–1791) was an Anglican clergyman, evangelist, and founder, along with his brother Charles, of the Methodist movement in the Church of England. In his home in London, which you can still visit today, there is a small prayer room off of which was John Wesley's bedroom. He was said to rise at 4:00 A.M every morning and spend four hours praying in this space.

Hear me, friends. I am not suggesting that you set your alarms for 4:00 A.M. and spend four hours in prayer. My alarm doesn't work before

7:00 during the school year and 8:30 during the summer. It's simply how I'm wired. We live in a broken world, and I accept the weakness of my flesh and my sincere aversion to early mornings. This is only one of the many reasons I need Jesus.

If you look into John Wesley's background, though, you'll undoubtedly read about a man who kept a rigid schedule and required those around him to do so as well. However, I see something more. John Wesley's prayer room afforded him a place devoid of distractions where he could sit, soak in God's Word, and pray.

For me, that place is my patio, where I sit every morning until my children find me. When I worked full-time at an office, I used to sit in the stairwell during lunch. Sometimes my special place is my car as I'm shuttling my children to and from various activities.

Do you have a special place where you can sit without distractions? Do you think a place like this is important for prayer? By the way, I asked my husband this question, hoping he would offer some really profound idea, which as a man of few words he does often share. I wasn't disappointed when Travis Bird responded with, "Of course. Even Superman needed a Fortress of Solitude." Nice.

HORATIO G. SPAFFORD

Horatio Spafford (1828–1888) was a prosperous lawyer and devout Presbyterian church elder. He and his wife, Anna, lived comfortably with their four young daughters in Chicago until their fortune evaporated in the Great Chicago Fire of 1871. Overnight, Horatio lost everything.

Yet Horatio and his family persevered. The family planned a trip abroad in late 1873, but business detained Horatio, so he sent his wife and daughters on a ship ahead of him. During the voyage, the SS *Ville du Havre* was struck by another vessel and sank within twelve minutes. All four of Horatio and Anna's daughters drowned, while his wife was pulled to safety. I can only imagine Horatio's immense devastation at receiving his wife's telegram that simply read, "Saved alone."

Horatio immediately left Chicago to bring his wife home. During the Atlantic crossing, the captain of the ship told Horatio when they were passing over the spot where his four daughters had perished. As the ship passed over the watery graves, Horatio wrote the hymn "It Is Well with My Soul."

I don't remember when I first heard the history of how this hymn came to be, but it always stuck with me. A modern-day Job, Horatio had every reason to sink into complete desolation. At the time he penned this hymn, Horatio and his wife had lost a total of five children. Yet in the darkest of moments, he still pursued God. He praised and prayed to God in the midst of unmovable mountains. *That* is faith.

God didn't promise a life full of clear skies and rainbows. He promised a life full of the redemptive power of his grace and the promise that we are never alone.

YOU

Yep, that's right. You are a modern-day prayer warrior, my friend. I could list dozens more inspiring names, but your name should be on that list as well as mine. We are *all* called to be prayer warriors. Paul tells us, "Never stop praying. Be thankful in all circumstances, for this is God's will for you who belong to Christ Jesus" (1 Thess. 5:17–18).

The enemy would have us believe that our words do not matter and that prayer is pointless. Lies! Our words and our prayers hold great power, and that truth scares the you-know-what out of Satan. There is a spiritual battle raging around us, and even though the war has already been won, the enemy is relentless in his pursuit of our families, our livelihoods, and quite honestly, of us. His sole purpose is to distract, divide, and destroy. As God's image bearers, we have the power and authority in Jesus's name to rebuke Satan and the force of evil he commands.

I assure you that we'll dig deeper into the creative exploration of prayer. However, I felt it was really important to provide a foundation in this chapter for what prayer is and why it's one of the most powerful blessings that God has given us.

Sandy Says

"Make the enemy quake by standing your spiritual ground. Wake up! Reach out! Be the spiritual warrior that you are called to be!"

THE HEART OF A WARRIOR

by the Rev. Stephen Ferguson

When Cat approached me to collaborate about the heart of a prayer warrior, my first thought was, "Why me?" While I am an intercessor and have at times been involved in spiritual warfare, I didn't consider myself a prayer *warrior*, unlike my late wife, Sandy, who was ten feet tall in the Spirit (and Cat's mom). However, through my military career as an infantry officer, I have come to understand and believe that the principles of physical warfare are transferable to the kingdom of God. In other words, battle in the spiritual realm is not very different from physical battle, except that, in spiritual warfare, the stakes are often much higher. So, let's look at what the heart of a warrior, particularly a prayer warrior, looks like.

While anyone engaged or experienced in warfare can be considered a warrior (stay with me on this), we often consider valor to be an essential quality of a *true* warrior. And probably with good reason, since the old *Merriam-Webster* dictionary says that valor is "strength of mind or spirit that enables a person to encounter danger with firmness." In other words, with personal bravery.

Our nation's highest award for valor is the Medal of Honor. Two valiant Medal of Honor recipients come to mind, both from World War II: Audie Murphy and Desmond Doss. Interestingly, one (Murphy) received the Medal for bravery as he killed enemy soldiers, and the other (Doss) received his as he saved fellow soldiers. Both exhibited incredible valor and should be considered warriors, yet Doss was a conscientious objector and refused to carry a gun, his only weapons being the Bible and prayer. Even under heavy enemy fire and wounded himself, Doss prayed after rescuing each wounded soldier, "Lord, just help me get one more." Prayer warriors may not usually have to dodge bullets, but they must have valiant hearts, because, as someone who likely spoke from experience once said, "Spiritual warfare ain't for sissies."

A prayer warrior's heart must also contain a deep love for one's fellow human beings, regardless of who they are and how they treat us. It is easy to love those who love us, but not so easy to love those who oppose or hurt us or our loved ones. Yet, Jesus says to love your enemies, do good to those who hate you, bless those who curse you, pray for those who mistreat you (Luke 6:27–28 NIV). Only when we see them as God's children can we have the type of love that allows us to step into the midst of spiritual battle on their behalf. The Apostle Paul reminds us that, without love, nothing else matters (1 Cor. 13). And that doesn't mean our love, but God's love for and in us. I saw a saying on the Internet recently: "You will never look into the eyes of someone God does not love and did not create." Kind of puts it in perspective, doesn't it?

Perhaps it should go without saying that faith should be at the foundation of a prayer warrior's heart. Bravery and love for others are important, to be sure, but without faith, prayer itself becomes insignificant and meaningless. The writer to the Hebrews says, "Now faith is the assurance of things hoped for, the conviction of things not seen" (Heb. 11:1 ESV). It is faith that allows our prayers to transcend all that the physical and spiritual worlds can throw at us, to assure us that God not only loves us and hears us, but that he has the power and desire to give us what we ask in accordance with his will.

Having said all that, let me gently add a caveat. In the military, all service members go through basic training, where they learn not only combat skills but such things as discipline, respect for authority and the chain of command, and survival skills. While all trainees learn the basics of combat and how to defend themselves and their fellow soldiers, only certain people are trained as combat soldiers, those who engage with and destroy the enemy. The same is true of the body of Christ.

As Christians, all of us are called to know the basics of the faith and to defend that faith when necessary. We are all called to a life of prayer and to intercede on behalf of others. However, before seeking to do battle with the enemy, make sure you are called to and trained for that ministry. In the meantime, I urge you to continue to pray and get to know your creator more intimately. Stay in the Word, and work on building your spiritual "muscles." Associate with like-minded Christians and learn from those who have gone before. Before you know it, you will be a prayer warrior.

Lord,

I lift up the people reading this prayer and ask you to speak peace and encouragement to their spirits. Remind them that, as your child, they have access to your throne room at all times, both for their own needs and for those of others. But, Lord, if you are calling them to be prayer warriors, to stand in the gap for those who cannot or will not come to you, give them an extra measure of your grace and protection, and equip them for the work of that ministry.

In Jesus's name we pray,

Amen

CHAPTER THREE

Who Is The Helper?

There is a navigation app on my phone I use regularly called Waze. It is a handy tool that looks for the fastest route, even if it means taking you a little off the beaten path. The developers of this app must have a wicked sense of humor, because like some other navigation apps, you can choose the voice that will tell you which way to go.

When I first downloaded the app, I chose the voice of Mr. T. I'm not even kidding. It was an option. As a kid growing up in the 1980s, you better believe I watched *The A-Team*. Mr. T was awesome, so hearing him tell me where to go? Epic. However, nothing prepared me for the first command that I heard in Mr. T's trademark gruff voice: "Turn left here, fool!" I had tears of laughter rolling down my face, but I still managed to follow his directions. Travis Bird made me change the voice in my Waze app not long after that maiden voyage. He said it *distracted* me instead of helping me, and I needed a guidance system that was a little subtler.

When I think about the Holy Spirit working in my life, sometimes he is subtle, but then sometimes he's not. Sometimes he's like Mr. T, telling me, "Turn left here, fool!" I have gotten more adept at listening to the Holy

Spirit's voice, but it's a work in progress. As my family can tell you, I have a tinge of a stubborn streak, so sometimes that still, soft voice in the wind isn't enough to get my attention.

IT'S NOT THAT KIND OF GHOST, ZAK BAGANS

Of the triune Godhead, the Holy Spirit has always been the most mysterious to me. God is God, and Jesus became man. That makes them a little easier to understand than the imagery of an ethereal Holy Ghost. As a child, I embraced the Bible stories about God, our creator, and his only Son, who became a man to save us from our sins. The Holy Spirit, though . . . I struggled with who he is and my relationship with him well into adulthood.

I'm being real, friends. I am your sister in Christ and a fellow sojourner in this walk of faith and by no means claim to be all-knowing. As my faith has grown and deepened, I have learned to lean more fully on the Holy Spirit and recognize him in the many roles he performs. However, if you struggle with understanding who the Holy Spirit is and what his purpose is, you are not alone. Theologian Sinclair Ferguson notes that many of us find the Holy Spirit to be more mystifying. He said, "The Spirit himself remains to many Christians an anonymous, faceless aspect of the divine being. Even the title 'Holy Spirit' evokes a different gamut of emotions from those expressed in response to the titles of 'Father' and 'Son.'"[1]

It is important to note that the Holy Spirit is just as present as the Father and the Son. Take a look at the first chapter of your Bible. The first time the Holy Spirit is mentioned is actually at the very beginning of Scripture: "In the beginning God created the heavens and the earth. The earth was formless and empty, and darkness covered the deep waters. And the Spirit of God was hovering over the surface of the waters" (Gen. 1:1–2).

We learn from Scripture that the Holy Spirit is a "he," a person, not an "it" (John 14:16–17). Scripture also portrays the Holy Spirit as having intellect, emotion, and will (1 Cor. 2:11; Rom. 15:30). This reflects the teaching of Scripture that the Holy Spirit is not an impersonal force or a mere attribute of God's power, but rather a person. The personal pronoun for the Holy Spirit and the fact that the Spirit possesses a will, knowledge, and emotion reveal his personhood (John 16:4b–11; Eph. 4:30).

We have a personal relationship with the Holy Spirit just as we have a personal relationship with the other two persons of the Holy Trinity. In Genesis 1:26, God says, "Let us make man in *our* image, after *our* likeness" (ESV; emphasis added). This verse reveals each person of the Trinity and reminds us of the importance to cultivate a relationship with God the Father, Jesus the Son, *and* the Holy Spirit. As image bearers of the Godhead, we share qualities with all three.

So how do we make contact with the Holy Spirit? Thankfully, we don't need Zak Bagans and the Ghost Adventures team or any other supernatural expert to help us. When Jesus took leave of his disciples, he said that he would ask the Father to send them the Holy Spirit. "And I will ask the Father, and he will give you another Helper, to be with you forever, even the Spirit of truth, whom the world cannot receive, because it neither sees him nor knows him. You know him, for he dwells with you and will be in you. I will not leave you as orphans; I will come to you" (John 14:16–18 ESV).

The Holy Spirit entered us when we made the choice to give our life to Christ and become a Christian. However, we need to continually ask the Holy Spirit to lead us, to guide us, to help us do the things God wants us to do. Scripture tells us this is the Holy Spirit's purpose in our walk of faith.

Through the Bible, we learn the Holy Spirit has many facets to his personality—the Comforter, the Advocate, the Counselor, the Helper. Let's unpack the many roles of the Holy Spirit. The following list shows several ways in which the Holy Spirit works in each of our lives. Take a few minutes, look up the attached verses, and write them in the spaces below.

The Holy Spirit speaks. (Acts 1:16)

The Holy Spirit prays. (Rom. 8:26–27)

The Holy Spirit teaches. (John 14:26)

The Holy Spirit convicts. (John 16:7–8)

The Holy Spirit commands. (Acts 8:29; Acts 11:12; Acts 13:2)

The Holy Spirit forbids. (Acts 16:6–7)

The Holy Spirit comforts. (John 14:16)

The Holy Spirit strengthens. (Eph. 3:16)

Sometimes the voice of the Holy Spirit is distinct and urgent, like a GPS telling us, "Turn left here!" Often, though, the Holy Spirit speaking feels like intuition, perhaps a nagging feeling that won't go away. In our human flesh, we can resist this feeling and choose in our free will to turn right when that voice urges us to turn left. That's right, friends. We have the power to resist the Holy Spirit (Ps. 106:33; Acts 7:51), and as a result, we can sometimes take a turn learning lessons through the School of Hard Knocks.

My husband and I had a serious disagreement several months ago. It was rough. We very seldom have arguments like this. I love this man, y'all. He has loved me through thick and thin (literally). However, in that moment, I wanted to *shut . . . him . . . down.* I knew he couldn't beat me in a verbal sparring match. There was a voice inside me saying, "Shut your mouth, Cat. Bite your tongue. Do not say what you're thinking. Do not. Do not. *Do not.*" I resisted that voice, opened my mouth, and delivered a painful blow. I knew the moment the words left my mouth that my husband was wounded, and just as I suspected, that last verbal swing ended the match—and no one won.

I hurt the other half of my heart when I resisted the Holy Spirit's nudging to shut my mouth. We cooled down, and I sought forgiveness for hurting him and for hurting *us*. For me, this is one of at least a dozen painful life lessons the Lord has allowed me to experience, and a not-so-gentle reminder that the Holy Spirit is present to help, not to hinder.

That's not to say God won't use our tough life lessons for some pretty awesome kingdom work, because I truly believe our God wastes nothing—positive or painful. My point is that we have the blessing and curse of free will, and God quite often allows us to live out the consequences of our choices. Nonetheless, these choices even when made in poor judgment cannot keep God from fulfilling his perfect plan. He sends the Holy Spirit to help us, to guide us, and to comfort us along the way.

A UNIQUE APPROACH

Just as we are made in the image of God, our Creator also gifted each and every one of us with qualities and characteristics that make us marvelously unique. And the way the Holy Spirit speaks to you is undeniably different than how he speaks to me.

My girls share qualities and characteristics of their dad and me, and while they may resemble one another, their personalities could not be more different. We approach conversations with each child in a way that best fits her temperament. One child responds better to close proximity, soft words, and physical touch, while another deeply resonates with blunt words and physical space to process a difficult conversation. Knowing our children as well as we do, Travis Bird and I speak to them how we know they will best receive what needs to be heard.

In much the same way, the Holy Spirit approaches each of us in the way we will hear him best. For some of us, that still, soft voice in the wind is sufficient. Others may require a little firmer nudge, along with "Turn left here!" There is no cookie-cutter way the Holy Spirit speaks, because we all hear and receive his voice differently.

The other day, I felt a strong nagging thought that I needed to check on a friend. Her name kept coming to mind, and I'll be honest: sometimes the introvert in me wins. I've been deep in my writing hidey-hole, and even when I'm not "in the hole," I don't love talking on the phone. With this friend's name on my mind most of the morning, I compromised with the Holy Spirit and sent my friend a Marco Polo video message instead of picking up the phone to call. It turns out she was really struggling. We spent the better part of the day exchanging messages, and because I listened to that nudging from the Holy Spirit, my friend received the encouragement she needed to hear.

The Holy Spirit knows each of us so intimately. God knows things about us that we don't even know about ourselves. You may be receptive to the Holy Spirit's voice as he is reflected in nature. Or perhaps you hear more clearly through worship. A friend of mine hears God through a certain number, which she sometimes sees on her clock, a license plate passing by on the road, or even the balance of her Starbucks card. The Holy Spirit knows how best to reach you.

Be willing to open your eyes and ears to the special way that God speaks to you specifically through the Holy Spirit, because he *is* speaking to you.

CONDEMNATION VERSUS CONVICTION

There is a difference between conviction and condemnation, and it is an important distinction. The enemy condemns. The Holy Spirit convicts. The voice that says, "You are a horrible mom." That's not of God. The Holy Spirit says, "There's a better way, and I love you." The Holy Spirit does not bring shame when he speaks.

It takes practice and a willingness to hear the Holy Spirit. Learn to know the voice. The voice of the Holy Spirit is hope*ful.* The voice of the enemy is hope*less.*

The enemy has had millennia to hone his craft of deceit and despair. He is cunning and clever, but you are not his. Your identity rests firmly on the foundation of Jesus Christ. When Jesus became man, he spoke truth. He brought hope. The gospel is called the Good News for a reason! However, Jesus spoke truth with love. That doesn't mean the truth won't sometimes be difficult to hear, but Jesus never delivered truth followed by, "You are not worthy. You are unloved. You are nothing." That is the enemy's battle cry.

The Holy Spirit speaks truth and love, and they are *always* spoken together. Again, that doesn't mean the truth won't sometimes be difficult to hear. The voice that says, "You are wrong, but you are still worthy. You are wounded, but you are still loved."—that's the voice of the Holy Spirit. He speaks with conviction full of truth and love, not condemnation and shame.

Listen for the difference and rebuke the enemy when he would speak louder than the Holy Spirit. When he would have you believe you are nothing, straighten your crown and remind the enemy that you are a daughter of the king.

WHEN WE DON'T HAVE WORDS

I mentioned that some of our prayers may sound childlike, and there is nothing wrong with this at all. Remember, Jesus tells us the kingdom belongs to such as these, to those who come to him like children (Matt. 19:14). However simplistic these prayers may seem, often they are born from a deep well within the soul. They're honest and raw. I think back to some of the rougher seasons I've lived through, and so many of my prayers uttered during those times were prayers of desperation. To be honest, there were times when I didn't have words at all. It was in those moments of despair and gut-wrenching pain that I prayed for God to give me the words to say, because I could think of none to offer him in prayer.

It's in those moments of "I don't know what to say, Lord" that the Holy Spirit intercedes for us. Romans 8:26–27 tells us that "the Holy Spirit helps us in our weakness":

> For example, we don't know what God wants us to pray for. But the Holy Spirit prays for us with groanings that cannot be expressed in words. And the Father who knows all hearts knows what the Spirit is saying, for the Spirit pleads for us believers in harmony with God's own will. (Rom. 8:26–27)

This is a powerful statement, friend. How many of us have fallen to our knees in utter defeat and surrender to the pain of life? And let's be real. Life does sometimes take us to our knees. Yet the Holy Spirit meets us there when we are weak, when we are without words, and he intercedes on our behalf before the throne of God. The groans that cannot be expressed in words are more compelling, because they convey even deeper emotion. That love the creator has for each and every one of us is also expressed in the tender yet fierce advocacy portrayed by the Holy Spirit on our behalf.

GOD HEARS PRAYERS WITHOUT WORDS

by Carey Scott

Sometimes we cannot find words to express what we're feeling. We may try to change things up as we pray, hoping a new position like kneeling down rather than sitting in our comfy chair or finding sacred space in nature instead of our prayer closet will invite in originality, but the words we desperately want to share with God still don't come. We're simply at a loss and feel hopeless and helpless. Stunted and shut down.

The Bible talks extensively about how our Father in Heaven hears our prayers and comes to rescue us. It tells us we don't have because we don't ask. Throughout its pages, we're continually reminded that the Lord answers prayers and that he is generous with his love and delight. But what happens when we can't pray in ways we normally do? What about those times we simply cannot form the right words or find our voice to speak out the words we do have?

I'm in one of those seasons right now. I'm in a kick-you-in-the-gut season where I'm just struggling to catch my breath. My hurt is so deep and my pain so real, and as a parent my immediate focus has to be on my children, who are experiencing their own complexity of emotions. Our world changed in an instant, and I'm just trying to keep our heads above water. And while I have a career wordsmithing thoughts and feelings into understandable sentences, I'm challenged to find a way to birth my pain into prayers.

I'm in a season of desperation on epic levels without words to describe it.

I want you to know these moments in life are real. Maybe you've experienced them before—maybe you're in one right now. There are times my prayer is a guttural moan that escapes from deep inside my soul. Other times I can only repeat the name of Jesus over and over and over again. Sometimes I sit in silence and weep, letting the tears stream down my cheeks and hoping God knows my heart. There are moments when I was only able to whisper the words *please* or *help* or *why*. Oh friend, I imagine you know exactly what I am talking about.

I truly believe these kinds of desperate prayers are precious to God. They come from such raw and honest places, where we've come to the end of ourselves and know he is our only hope. Scripture tells us that God is close to the brokenhearted, and I believe he has a very special place in his heart for those times his children cry out from such deep pain. He isn't looking for perfect words. He isn't waiting for us to share our feelings by following rules or formats. Instead, the Bible says he knows the depth of our hearts because he designed us and created the intense range of emotions we were meant to experience in life.

He knows *everything* about you and me.

And that means he already knows the glorious complexities of what you're feeling. He understands your pain better than you do. You're crying out to a God who already has a plan in place to intervene, restore, heal, define, remind, transform, and surround you with his life-changing love. And it's in those times—especially, I would imagine—that he wants to hear from you.

So I'm encouraging you to be free to pray with imperfection. Be real with the Lord in your moments of pain. Moan, weep, scream, or repeat the name of Jesus in a whisper. Sit before God with no words at all and be confident that he sees the entirety of your emotions and feelings. There are just some seasons where we cannot find words—and we don't have to.

It's in these hard moments we can trust that God knows it all.

BEING FRUITY IS A GOOD THING

How can you tell if you're being led by the Holy Spirit? By the *fruit* of your life—your attitudes and actions. Galatians 5:22–23 says, "The fruit of the Spirit is love, joy, peace, patience, kindness, goodness, faithfulness, gentleness, self-control" (ESV). Are these things evident in your life?

Friends, the Holy Spirit doesn't give us seeds. He gives us fruit, and fruit takes time to grow. Remember the lesson of prayer from Elijah? Be bold and ask God for these things. Then ask the Holy Spirit to help these things grow within you. If you need patience, ask for it. Kindness? Ask for it. However, be prepared. When you pray for fruits of the Spirit, these gifts usually come through opportunities to practice them.

Let's take kindness, for example. My mom once told me about a lunch she had with a group of her friends. They were there to celebrate a gal pal who was facing a particularly difficult season. Her husband had left her, and without a job herself, she had no idea how she was going to provide for her two young children. The sole purpose of their gathering was to love on this sweet friend and encourage her.

Their waitress that day was incredibly rude, so much so that even my mom agreed her tip should reflect her terrible behavior and service. My mom's friend, who they were there to honor that day, felt compassion for the waitress and decided to leave all the money she had in her wallet on the table, which she waited to do until all the other ladies had begun to leave the restaurant. My mom realized she left something at the table and went back only to hear the waitress complaining to her friend about the meager coins that had been left on the table. My mom's friend literally gave all she had, and this waitress was clearly unhappy and had no problem telling my mom's friend that the tip was offensive.

My mom was known for her kindness, but you did not want to make her angry. It's safe to say, Sandy was *hot* that day. She said she opened her mouth to give the sassafras waitress a piece of her mind but her friend spoke first. Even in the midst of an encounter with a foul-tempered person, my mom's friend gently explained it was all she had to leave and that she hoped the waitress's day would improve and that God would bless her mightily. Friends, even though the waitress stormed away, kindness was shared.

Perhaps the waitress was having a horrible day. My mom said she hugged her friend and resisted the urge to follow the waitress so she could give her a swift kick in the pants. However, she realized her friend had showed the mean-tongued server the face of Jesus in spite of how horribly she had been treated. She was cultivating the fruit of kindness within her spirit.

When you allow the Holy Spirit to cultivate these fruits within you, which also means asking for opportunities to practice them, think about how powerful of a testimony your actions become to believers and nonbelievers alike. I get it. It's not always easy. In fact, these opportunities seldom are. Yet we shouldn't show exception to when or how we lend kindness or any other fruits of the Spirit. Even to the person who cut you off in traffic. Or the salesperson who rudely asked you what you want. Kindness is going out of your way to snail mail a card to someone who needs an encouraging word, even if it means going out of your way to buy a card and then braving the seventh circle of hell (also known as the post office) to get it mailed. It's offering to let someone else go in line before you. Kindness is reflected in small acts as well as large ones.

Can you imagine a world where we focused our energy on cultivating the fruits of the Spirit within one another and ourselves?

Sandy Says

"I can't wait to hear what God through his Holy Spirit has revealed to you. Please share with others! You never know how what you share will impact someone's journey."

SPEAKING OF THAT GENTLE NUDGING

I've wanted to write this book for years. When it finally came to fruition, I prayed about a way to make this book more personal and relatable to every person who looked within its pages. I felt the Holy Spirit's nudging to include contributions from friends who live their faith boldly and pray even bolder. I am deeply honored to share their hearts. May you be blessed by their words.

THE HOLY SPIRIT, MY HELPER

by Jen Ferguson

My husband had been sick for almost a year with an autoimmune disease. We'd been fighting it with medicine, with diet and exercise, and, of course, with prayer. We were at a pretty depressing point in the battle where nothing seemed to be working to decrease his symptoms or to facilitate healing. Especially frustrated one morning, I turned to my usual stress reliever—running. As one who struggles with anxiety, it is often helpful to release my nervous energy so that I can more clearly hear God. Being out in nature gives me a glimpse of the Holy Spirit.

When someone says the words *God* or *Jesus*, there are often images we conjure up in our minds of what each of them looks like. When you say *Holy Spirit*, it's a little more difficult to construct a picture. And yet, this is the being that Jesus gave to us as he left this earth. This is the very being who brings us into union with the Father and the Son, who reminds us of the truth, counsels us, comforts us, strengthens us, and guides us. We have to train our eyes to see the Holy Spirit and his movements—in the breeze against our face, in the comfort of a warm blanket, in the creative intricacies of beauty in flowers and mountains and people around us. All of these things (and more) are constant reminders of that presence, of the prominence he wants to have in our life because of God's great love and passion for us.

It was this great love and passion of which I needed reminding. The struggle with chronic illness can feel isolating and mind-numbing. How can you defeat something doctors don't even really understand? The trial-and-error mentality can feel overwhelmingly hopeless.

There is plenty of space for despair to creep in. But this also means there is plenty of space for the Holy Spirit to bring life. Running that day felt like running with God. The Holy Spirit took my authentic cries of frustration and led me to this simple statement: Show me how to pray.

You might think that this would have been my natural posture. I've been following Jesus for twenty-eight years. Surely I would trust the One who created my husband to know how to fix him. But it is so easy to get wrapped up in how the world approaches problems, to be limited by our humanness. Sometimes—many times—we have to come to the end of ourselves in order to see the beginning of God.

As my feet pounded pavement that morning, as I realized both the world's and my own limitations, my body responded to the Holy Spirit's presence. Romans 8:26–28 became personal:

> Meanwhile, the moment we get tired in the waiting, God's Spirit is right alongside helping us along. If we don't know how or what to pray, it doesn't matter. He does our praying in and for us, making prayer out of our wordless sighs, our aching groans. He knows us far better than we know ourselves, knows our pregnant condition, and keeps us present before God. That's why we can be so sure that every detail in our lives of love for God is worked into something good. (MSG)

When we can't figure things out, when we can't understand, when we don't know what to do, when we feel alone, when we don't know if we have what it takes to overcome—this is why Jesus sent the Holy Spirit! He is adamantly helping us keep our circumstances from tainting how we see God, to bring truth against the lies, and to bring comforting words to calm our anxious hearts. He helps us address our sin so we may access God's relentless forgiveness and freedom. He gives us peace where there is strife, gentleness in harsh conditions, goodness and kindness in the face of evil.

In his letter to the Galatians, Paul says, "So I say, let the Holy Spirit guide your lives. Then you won't be doing what your sinful nature craves" (5:16). My sinful nature wants to control and complain and doubt. But the Holy Spirit wants to teach me a different way to live, a way free from anxiety and hopelessness. The Holy Spirit took my groans that day and gave me new words. He gave me creative ways to pray to address the illness that had gripped my husband. He taught me to look beyond the surface problems and to probe deeper, to see the connections our physical bodies have to our emotions and to our souls.

This experience beautifully encapsulates what the Holy Spirit does—lead us deeper into Jesus, deeper into his truth, deeper into the callings he has given us.

Holy Spirit,

Thank you for being a willing participant in all of our lives, including the person reading this prayer right now. May well all know that with you, we never have to navigate life by ourselves. Help us receive the wisdom and power you long give us and prepare our hearts for where you'll lead us. May we know that you are always good, always kind, and always want to fulfill the amazing plans you have for us. With you, we are never alone.

Amen

CHAPTER FOUR

DOES GOD HEAR AND ANSWER OUR PRAYERS?

When I was seven months pregnant with my youngest daughter, my husband was laid off from work. I can still remember him calling me that dreary February morning. My heart fell as I listened to his words. I could hear his tears.

Not again. Please, God. Not again.

This was his fourth layoff in five years, two of those occurring when I was seven months pregnant with each child. We were devastated. I was in the midst of a high-risk pregnancy and had been ordered off and on bed rest since my first trimester. At that time, I was off bed rest and back at work, but that did not last long.

One week after my husband lost his job, I was admitted to the hospital, where I would remain until our daughter was born. We were crazy with worry as to how we were going to make it. In a matter of two weeks, we had gone from a two-income family to surviving on my short-term disability. My mom came to Austin to stay with our older daughter while my husband spent his days and nights at the hospital with me. We prayed and waited.

Our youngest daughter was born nearly six weeks early by emergency C-section. The doctors had to put me under general anesthesia, because I was too swollen to insert a needle in my back for an epidural. A needle in the back was too risky. My husband and I had already agreed that no matter what happened, he would stay with the baby. My mom would stay with me.

After making arrangements for our older daughter, my mom arrived at the hospital to await the arrival of our newest family member. Two pregnant women were in emergency surgeries, another mom-to-be and me. My husband was waiting just outside the door of my operating room, and my mom was in the waiting room.

As soon as our daughter was born, my husband rushed alongside of the neonatal doctors and nurses as they begin to work on our baby girl. She could not breathe on her own, and they quickly whisked her away to another floor with my husband in tow.

My mom sat and waited. She waited until nurses came out of both operating rooms.

"How did it go?" one nurse asked.

"She didn't make it," was the sad response.

For years after, my mom would say time stopped for her. She had no idea which operating room I was in, and in that moment, she prayed fervently for God to perform a miracle. My obstetrician came out a short time later, and my mom said she just sat and wept. I was very sick, she said, but I was going to be OK. Her heart wept with joy that I was fine, yet she also wept tears of sorrow for the family of the other mom-to-be whose lives were irrevocably changed that night.

By the morning after our daughter was born, my husband had not slept in two days. Our baby girl was on one floor in the neonatal intensive care unit, and I was on another floor of the hospital still floating in and out of consciousness. His phone rang, and he let it go to voicemail. Bless his heart. He was beyond exhausted and finally collapsed on a mattress the medical staff brought into my room.

When he was able to check messages later, the call he had received was from an architecture firm with an offer to hire him. My husband had interviewed months prior to this call with absolutely no communication since. Our daughter was less than twenty-four hours old when my husband accepted a position with the firm where he just celebrated his thirteenth anniversary.

God answered our prayers.

In those first few years following the birth of our second daughter, our budget was *lean*. My husband and I prayed following the birth of our second child about whether or not I should return to work. Daycare was going to cost about what I was earning each month, and after much discussion and prayer, we took a step in faith. I quit my job.

On paper, it did not look like our budget should work. In fact, it was downright scary. Yet, somehow, some way, we were able to pay our bills each month. Our insurance company sends dividend checks to members every year, and they usually arrive around Christmas. That first December after our second daughter was born, the check was *to the penny* what we needed to pay our electric bill.

THE SUNDAY HOUSE PRAYER

I remember confiding to my friend Nancy how stressful our lives felt, how we worried every month as we wondered how we were going to manage to pay our bills. This is when she told me about the Sunday House prayer.

Nancy, too, had weathered stormy seasons. My friend was going through a divorce, and her two children were in high school at the time. Her relationship with her husband had been difficult. Her heart was battered and bruised, but she still trusted in God's plan. She trusted in the power of prayer, and she encouraged me to do the same.

My friend's husband had left once before when their children were much younger. They had moved their family out of state to follow a wonderful job opportunity, built their dream home, and then watched the world fall apart. When her husband left, my friend moved back to Texas with a broken heart and two devastated children. Her husband had been the breadwinner. She had no idea where they were going to live or what she was going to do.

A family member called my friend and told her about a place called the Sunday House, a small house on a big piece of property just outside of Houston. It was available for rent. A couple of weeks before she was to see the house, she grabbed a pen and paper and sat down with her son and daughter. She asked them to tell her what they thought would make the perfect place to live. No request was too big or unrealistic for God. They took turns and added to their list of what would make their new home a wonderful place. They wrote down their boldest hearts' desires.

A blue house with a pony in the back. A basketball court. A front porch with a swing.

Nancy held her son and daughter's hands as they prayed over their house list and then tucked the paper into their Bible. A few weeks later, Nancy said another quick prayer and then ventured out to see the Sunday House. When she arrived, she stood and stared. There in front of her sat a blue house with a pony in the back, a basketball court, and a front porch with a swing.

God had shown up in a big way, in a way only God can. That began what would become the Sunday House prayer, and my friend shared this special way to pray in which we lay our dreams boldly at God's feet—just like Elijah (1 Kings 18:36–38). Each year since then, my husband and I sit down and write our own Sunday House prayer. No request is too big or unrealistic for God. We hold hands, pray over our list, and tuck it away in one of our Bibles. At the end of each year, we pull out the list and see how God has answered our prayers.

Some things on our Sunday House prayer have been there for years. Sometimes God answers our prayers quickly and says, "Yes." Sometimes, in God's perfect provision, he says, "No." Other times, he says, "Not yet."

GOD ALWAYS ANSWERS, EVEN IF THE ANSWER IS NO

Our God is a God of love, but he is also deeply personal. We've reiterated how each and every one of us is created with purpose out of love, carefully knit in our mothers' wombs (Ps. 139:13). As our creator, Jesus tells us that God knows our needs before we do (Matt. 6:8). God is also holy and wise, and he knows what is best for us, what will lead us to holiness rather than to sin. "But anyone who does not love does not know God, for God is love. We know how much God loves us, and we have put our trust in his love" (1 John 4:8, 16).

The Bible tells us that God delights in his creation (Gen. 1; Ps. 104), and he longs for a relationship with us. The apostle John wrote that we are to *love God because he first loved us* (1 John 4:19). Prayer is critical to our relationship with God, because it allows us to interact with him in a meaningful way. We are encouraged to come regularly and boldly before his throne: "So let us come boldly to the throne of our gracious God. There we will receive his mercy, and we will find grace to help us when we need it most." (Heb. 4:16).

Does God answer prayers? Yes. He does. Always. No prayer is too great or too small, and the Bible is chock-full of examples of how God responds to these petitions and earnest requests.

HANNAH

In the Old Testament, we meet Hannah. She was a second wife, barren and ridiculed because of her inability to have children. She prayed to God, asking for him to bless her with a son, which she promised to give back to him (1 Sam. 1:11). God heard her cry. In addition to her son Samuel, who became one of Israel's greatest prophets, Hannah also gave birth to three other sons and two daughters.

KING HEZEKIAH

King Hezekiah offers another wonderful example of prayer for us. When the powerful Assyrian King Sennacherib laid siege to Jerusalem, King

Hezekiah encouraged his people to keep their faith in God. He asked them to pray for delivery from their enemy (2 Kings 19:4). The angel of the Lord struck down eighty-five thousand Assyrian soldiers, which compelled the rest of the enemy's army to return home without a fight. King Hezekiah's people were saved. Woo-hoo!

PETER

We remember Peter as one of Jesus's twelve disciples and a leader of the early Christian church. After the Ascension of Jesus, Peter, along with the other disciples, worked diligently to share the gospel with as many people as possible. This didn't always go over well with the people in power, and Peter was arrested on more than one occasion.

After his third arrest (Acts 12:1–19), Peter found himself chained and under the guard of sixteen soldiers (Acts 12:4). Peter prayed, and while he was imprisoned, an angel appeared in Peter's jail cell to lead him out of the prison, through the doors, and past the guards. Peter arrived at Mary's house, where the church was gathered to pray, and they were all surprised to see him. Peter himself was baffled that God had answered his prayer so quickly.

God does not always answer our prayers as we ask him or in the timeframe we hope for. While he was on earth, Jesus modeled for us how we should talk with God by praying to God himself. On the night Jesus was betrayed and arrested, he prayed to his Father, asking for a reprieve from the torture and death he knew awaited him.

"And going a little farther he fell on his face and prayed, saying, "My Father, if it be possible, let this cup pass from me; nevertheless, not as I will, but as you will" (Matt. 26:39 ESV). Look how Jesus ended his prayer. Even though he dreaded what was to come, Jesus concluded his prayer with a statement of complete obedience to God—"not as I will, but as you will."

One month before my fortieth birthday, my mom was diagnosed with stage four pancreatic cancer. Her prognosis was grim, but our family rallied and prayed for complete healing. She fought that awful disease for nearly nine months before God answered our prayers. He just did not answer them the way we thought he would. At noon on June 21, 2017, my mom stepped from her hospice bed into the arms of Jesus. God had answered our prayers and healed her completely. She was whole once more.

Throughout her illness, I heard my mom say repeatedly how much she wanted to get well, to travel with my dad, to see her grandbabies graduate from high school and then college, and to watch them marry and have children of their own. Yet she prayed, "Not as I will, but as you will, Lord." She trusted in God's perfect provision not just for her life, but for the lives of her loved ones as well.

Our hearts were broken when my mom passed from this earthly world, but the truth remains. God answered our prayers of healing for my mom. She is happy and whole, and she no longer feels the pain of the awful disease that wracked her body.

God *always* answers prayers, even if the answer is no or not yet. God answered yes to Hannah, King Hezekiah, and Peter's prayers, while he said no to Jesus's prayer to avoid a painful death. Regardless of God's timing or his answer, he listens, hears, and responds to the petitions we lay before him.

Sandy Says

"We need to understand that sometimes our hope deferred is so God's will can be fulfilled. God always means it for our good. Be encouraged!"

ARE YOU THERE, GOD? IT'S ME, MARGARET

You may remember the story of Gideon and how he tested the Lord. Gideon was an Israelite leader introduced to us in Judges 6. God directed him to gather the Israelite troops to defeat the Midianite invaders, but Gideon wasn't so sure it was really God's voice he was hearing. He prayed and asked God for a sign to prove that what Gideon was hearing was indeed coming from God. Gideon laid a piece of wool outside overnight and asked God to make it wet while keeping the surrounding dirt dry. God did as Gideon asked, and in the morning the fleece was wet enough to produce a bowl of water when it was wrung out (Judg. 6:38).

Still, Gideon wasn't sure he was actually hearing God. He needed another sign. Again he laid a piece of wool outside, this time asking God to keep the fleece dry while making the surrounding dirt wet (Judg. 6:39). Again God answered Gideon's prayer (Judg. 6:40). Finally, Gideon was convinced it was God's voice he was hearing, which meant the nation of Israel would have victory over their enemy as promised by the angel of the Lord in Judges 6:14–16.

Gideon's hesitant faith reminds me of a book I read as a young girl, *Are You There God? It's Me, Margaret* (by Judy Blume). In the book, a young girl named Margaret struggles with her faith, having been raised by a Christian mother and Jewish father, neither of whom had taught her really anything about either religion. She tackles the topic of people's religious beliefs for a school assignment in the hope of figuring out what she believes along the way. As the story unfolds, we see Margaret experiencing the ups and downs of a young girl's life while trying to decide if there really is a God.

OK, you may be thinking, "Cat, how can you even begin to compare a grown man of faith from the Bible with a fictional not-sure-what-she-believes adolescent girl?" Friends, they were both doubters. Even though Margaret is a fictional character, she reflects the same doubts and insecurities we all inevitably feel at some point as humans living in a broken world. Gideon knew there was a God, but he didn't trust that God could speak to him. He couldn't discern God's voice or his presence. Margaret faced the same problem. They both doubted him.

Remember that we are innately wired to yearn for community, and something inside of our spirit recognizes there is a space within us that can only be filled by God. At the beginning of this chapter, I talked about the season of my marriage and motherhood where God was quiet. Storms were raging, and I cried out for him to still those crashing waves. What did I hear? More storms. More crashing waves. I doubted God when I couldn't feel or hear him. I felt abandoned.

I can think of several instances of my life where I questioned God's presence, wondering where in the world he was and why I couldn't sense him. In seasons that felt so dark and grim, I cried out, "Lord, why are you silent? Why can't I hear you?"

I wanted to say, "Are you there, God? It's me, Cat."

It's not that God wasn't there. He is ever-present with us. Nothing about the great I Am changes, which we should find comforting, especially in the midst of stormy seasons of life. Isaiah says, "From eternity to eternity I am God. No one can snatch anyone out of my hand. No one can undo what I have done" (43:13).

In those stormy seasons, I've found it is especially difficult to trust God's perfect timing, too. Sometimes I can sense God moving in the present, but often I see him best when I look back at all he's done around me. That's another reason I think that George Müller recording his answered prayers was such a brilliant idea, and that's also part of the reason the Sunday House prayer is so powerful. We give God glory for moving in a mighty way—especially when he calms the storms and those crashing waves—and then it becomes abundantly clear just how powerful his presence remains.

A SILENT CONFESSION

by Bekah Pogue

I'm a words person. A sit-down-and-listen-to-you and process-all-the-things-together person. I make sense of life by asking and hearing words. For much of my younger life, I weighed my value by collecting feedback from others, specifically my parents or authority figures, and then I co-dependently adjusted my behavior for the goal of relational and emotional connection.

Oh, I get applause when I perform? Note to self: perform more.

Oh, I get attention when I'm happy? Note to self: don't let my sadness leak out.

Oh, I get weird blank stares when I ask a million questions? Note to self: don't ask so many questions.

I adjusted my behavior like a runaway yo-yo, unaware that I was allowing verbal words—whether true or untrue—to dictate my independence, confidence, and ability to listen to God's voice first. You can imagine a soul who values communication—any words, really—who prays, only to be met with silence and, well, that surfaces a lot of ugly. Ugly like, *God, where the heck are you and can you please turn this thing on?* "This thing" happens to be whatever is close to me at the time, like a glass of wine or a couch pillow. I'm obviously tapping it like a microphone because there are no sounds coming from sweet Jesus.

So I talk more and get bossier. *Helllოooo?* It's quite pathetic, really. Imagine a stomping toddler, and there you have it when I'm wanting to hear God's voice and nada. *Zilch. Nothin' but silence.*

After I put on a recent Pasture experience (a women's gathering for the purpose of soul nourishment and connection), I received a text the following morning. "I hope you are celebrating all that God is doing," the vibration whispered. I paused from stirring cheesy eggs and glanced at my phone again and read: "I hope you are celebrating all that God is doing."

You know my first gut response?

What is God doing?

Other than a beautiful evening and a room brimming with women the night before, I haven't heard a word about last night's Pasture experience. *What is he doing?*

Followed by an honest interior question: *Do I have to hear about him working to know that he is present?*

It makes sense that since I value verbal processing, I subconsciously expect verbal feedback or words pointing to growth, or a valued experience, or a story about how God worked to weight the truth that the experience actually mattered. But are words essential to what God believes is best for our growth? For our journey? Do we need words to reinforce that following where we feel stirred to go or create, or where we work, or how we love cements that we made the right decision? Isn't it enough that an experience mattered to me? To you? That we believe it deep down in our toes?

What if our very expectation and what we hope for is met with silence? And what if silence is the very way we are to grow? What if no words or stories come our way—from people but mostly from God—to invite surrender, to release the expectation of hearing anything at all? I'm exploring my own silent journey with God. I know the feelings—all the feelings—and am seeing the beauty that emerges when I can't hear the good Lord but desperately want to.

I'm learning that God's gracious silence is a hidden gift.

Think of when you most need to be fully known and loved all the more. For me, it's usually when I'm venting or processing aloud or asking questions to make sense of life. What is it we most need in these moments? A safe space to be heard, right? And this is the gracious kind gift God offers in his silence. Because he can't listen to us and talk at the same time. So, as a good parent does, he listens. He scoots up close and pulls us near and listens. And then he listens longer. Because the honest, deeper vulnerabilities emerge after sacred silence. I'm learning that the times I most crave his voice are when he offers not his words, but his comfort instead. His protection. His wings (Ps. 91). His nearness of Spirit.

What if God is holding us so tight, so proud and Papa-bear huggy, with his strong hands wrapped around our ears and our faces pressed into his barrel of a chest, that we hear not words, but the gentle beating vibrations of his heart? What if his nearness is more sacred than a verbal response? What if we know our best efforts are rewarded by a proud praise of an embrace?

From a Father to his daughter. Pats included.

CREATIVE CONTEMPLATION

Today, spend some time thinking about your own Sunday House prayer and use the space at the end of this chapter to write down your thoughts. Remember, no prayer is too great or too small. Part of trusting God with our prayers means also trusting his sovereignty and timing, knowing he wants the very best for us. If you have a few extra minutes, grab your colored pencils and doodle on the colorable clock art as you contemplate God's faithfulness to listen, hear, and respond to your prayers.

"Pray so big and so often that when God meets you at heaven's gates, he says, 'Kid, you kept me very busy.'"

—AUTHOR UNKNOWN

God,

For the reader in a season of silence, I offer this prayer over her right now. We confess that we want to hear your voice and silence feels scary. In our longing for your words, your direction, your leading, your advice, turn us now to your nearness, your comfort, your arms wrapped tightly around each and every one of us. Echo in our spirits the truth that you will not leave us or forsake us. You began a good work in each of us and will see it through to completion. Give us steadfast patience in this space of silence. Root in us a compassion to know you are near even when we can't decipher your voice. Envelop us in grace when we are weary from the journey. You, Father, know what each of us needs. And though we may not understand, may we trust that your silence is refining us to know you deeper and more intimately.

Amen

—PRAYER OFFERING BY BEKAH POGUE

Be PATIENT
I hear YOU
Yes!
TRUST God's TIMING
Not Yet
No
Ask in Jesus's NAME
For everything there is a season, and a TIME for every matter under heaven...
ECCLESIASTES 3:1 ESV

PART TWO

How We Pray

"TRUE PRAYER IS AN APPROACH OF THE SOUL BY THE SPIRIT OF GOD TO THE THRONE OF GOD. IT IS NOT THE UTTERANCE OF WORDS, IT IS NOT ALONE THE FEELING OF DESIRES, BUT IT IS THE ADVANCE OF THE DESIRES TO GOD, THE SPIRITUAL APPROACH OF OUR NATURE TOWARD THE LORD OUR GOD. TRUE PRAYER IS NEITHER A MERE MENTAL EXERCISE NOR A VOCAL PERFORMANCE. IT IS FAR DEEPER THAN THAT—IT IS SPIRITUAL TRANSACTION WITH THE CREATOR OF HEAVEN AND EARTH."

—CHARLES SPURGEON

CHAPTER FIVE

A FRAMEWORK FOR PRAYER

So far, we've unpacked the *what* and *why* of prayer. Now let's turn our focus to the *how*. If we flip to the Gospel of Luke, Jesus provides a framework for how we should pray. In this passage of Scripture, Jesus taught us the Lord's Prayer.

> Now Jesus was praying in a certain place, and when he finished, one of his disciples said to him, "Lord, teach us to pray, as John taught his disciples." And he said to them, "When you pray, say: 'Father, hallowed be your name. Your kingdom come. Give us each day our daily bread, and forgive us our sins, for we ourselves forgive everyone who is indebted to us. And lead us not into temptation.'" (Luke 11:1–4 ESV)

The Lord's Prayer is more than a framework for prayer, though. It's also a framework for a relationship with Jesus. If prayer is an open, honest conversation with God, the Lord's Prayer provides a solid foundation for us to build upon. Take a look at the Lord's Prayer as found in *The 1979 Book of Common Prayer*:

Our Father in heaven,
hallowed be your Name,
your kingdom come,
your will be done,
on earth as in heaven.
Give us today our daily bread.
Forgive us our sins
as we forgive those who sin against us.
Save us from the time of trial,
and deliver us from evil.
For the kingdom, the power,
and the glory are yours,
now and for ever. Amen.[1]

The Lord's Prayer is arguably the best-known, most beloved prayer of the church. However, do you think it is possible to become overfamiliar with the words? Do you ever recite them without thinking, the memorized prayer having become a ritualistic habit that holds no genuine meaning? I am guilty of this, friends. In my busy, full-of-distractions life, sometimes I find my mouth reciting the words while my mind wanders elsewhere.

PERSONALIZING THE LORD'S PRAYER

If you find yourself uttering these beautifully memorized words without pausing to embrace all that they mean, I encourage you to reexamine the Lord's Prayer more slowly. Take time to personalize this love letter to God, maybe something like the following.

Our Father in heaven

Lord God, creator of the heavens and earth, thank you for all that you do. You literally spoke our world into being (Gen. 1:3), and you stretched the northern sky over empty space and hung the earth on nothing (Job 26:7). Even when our earthly relationships fall short, you are forever faithful. Yahweh, you are my Father in heaven, and I love you.

hallowed be your Name

You and you alone are God. I have no other gods before you, Lord (Exod. 20:3). You delivered Moses and the Israelites from slavery in Egypt

(Exod. 12:51), and you continued to rescue them time and time again. You also rescue me when I stray from the path of faith, which I am prone to do time and time again. You are my rock and my fortress (Ps. 18:2), Lord God; you are worthy of praise, and I praise your holy name, the name above all names.

your kingdom come

Abba, Father, I truly believe that Scripture bears your breath and every Word is true. Scripture tells us one day your kingdom will come to welcome me and all other believers to our new home (Rev. 5:10). I rejoice in that truth, Lord, and look forward to the day when Jesus returns. Until then, I will strive to live my faith out loud so that when I do stand before you on my day of judgment, you may say, "Well done, good and faithful servant."

your will be done

I struggle against the ways of the world, Father God. We live in a time and place that would have us believe we *deserve* worldly fame and riches. The enemy works hard to make us believe the lie that true happiness may be found by attaining earthly pleasures. I know you have plans for me, Lord: plans to give me hope and a future (Jer. 29:11), and the heavenly place you have set aside for me cannot be measured by earthly standards. It is priceless. Help me pray as Jesus modeled for us, "Not as I will, but as you will" (Luke 22:42). Help me trust in your will and your way.

on earth as in heaven

Lord, help me be more like Jesus. I want to love and praise you on earth and in heaven. You made me with purpose, care, and detail in my mother's womb (Ps. 139:13). I long to walk in fellowship with you as Adam and Eve did in the Garden of Eden (Gen. 3:8). Help me seek you first in all things.

Give us today our daily bread

Lord, every day I have is a gift from you. You control the days, the nights, the sun, the moon, the stars, and the weather. You are in total control of the universe, and I praise you for how perfectly it all fits together. You are so faithful, God, to provide for my needs and those that I love. Thank you for the food on my family's table, the roof over our heads, and the clothes that cover our bodies. You give breath and life to each and every one of us. Please continue to bless us, and if it is your will, Lord, please provide the means for us to bless others. Help us remember those who struggle, and light within our bellies a fire to serve those less fortunate. Help us love one another as you have loved us.

Forgive us our sins
Oh, sweet mercy. Lord, I fail you daily. In the weakness of my flesh, I sometimes choose the way of the world. These choices are often reflected in my thoughts, words, and deeds. Forgive me, Father. Thank you for loving me so much that you sent your one and only Son to save me, to save my family, to save us all. You know me better than I know myself, so please forgive my sins, known and unknown. Give me strength, as only you can, to make better choices that honor you and help draw others closer to you. Help me never lose sight of your power and my thankfulness for your unfathomable grace.

as we forgive those who sin against us
Malice has a shrewd memory for hurts but an awful memory for kindness. Lord, please give me a forgiving spirit to love others who hurt me and those I love. None of us deserve grace, but you have extended this gift to each and every one of us regardless of our sins and broken human nature. Help me love deeply and unconditionally so that others may reach for the grace that you have freely given to us all.

Save us from the time of trial
Oh, Lord. Thank you for your endless grace and the sometimes not-so-subtle nudging of the Holy Spirit. I want to follow you, Lord. Please help me humbly follow wherever you lead. I surrender to you, Father. When I am in control, there are so many wrong directions I can choose. Give me the strength, determination, and encouragement I need to trust you in all things and with everyone I hold dear.

and deliver us from evil
No one understands the craftiness of the enemy better than you, Lord. He is relentless in his pursuit of your flock, seeking to steal souls and attack the faithful where they are weakest. Scripture tells us that even Jesus

was tempted by the enemy (Matt. 4:1–11). I cannot resist him on my own, but I trust you to give me the strength to overcome any of the enemy's attacks. Draw me closer to you, Lord God, and away from the enemy's snare. Sustain me through seasons of battle, and help me stand firm when it is my turn to stand in the gap and fight the enemy on behalf of others. Help me wield the sword of the Spirit like a ninja, and instill in me a deep hunger to absorb your Word daily. My hope rests firmly in you, God.

For the kingdom, the power, and the glory are yours
Father, your home is where I want my home to be. You are the God I love and the One whom I long to know deeper. You are all-powerful, God (Rev. 19:6). As the Great I Am, you have power to love, to forgive, to care for each and every part of your creation, to hear those who cry out to you, to help those in need, to rebuke those who disobey. You are in control. I worship you and you alone, and I am so very thankful for the gift of salvation. Everything I have is thanks to you, Lord.

now and for ever
You are the unchangeable One who was, who is, who is to come, and who will always be (Mal. 3:6). Your Word stands forever (Isa. 40:8). All honor and glory be to you. I love you, God. I am yours.

Amen.

This is just an example of a way you can personalize the Lord's Prayer. I hear folks often say how unqualified they feel to pray, and I get it. I felt that way, too, until I realized I was overcomplicating something that was really rather simple. As the One who created us, God already knows our hearts intimately. Try not to get tripped up in making pretty words. Speak from your spirit, and the words will come.

Also, remember the Lord's Prayer is a template for our own conversations with God. If you look back, Jesus shows us how prayer begins and ends with praise and worship. In the Lord's Prayer, we seek God's forgiveness and ask him to give us a compassionate heart toward others. We ask for God to provide for our basic needs. As you recite the Lord's Prayer moving forward, I encourage you to pause and think through how this beautiful offering to God applies personally to you.

WHERE DO I SCHEDULE PRAYER IN MY HAPPY PLANNER?

Oh, happy day! Friends, I *love* office supplies and anything that helps me feel organized. One of my very favorite days each year is the day my new Happy Planner arrives, and I spend hours filling it with color-coded dates and stickers. Then there's the utter bliss of school supply shopping and the organizing of binders and such. My husband becomes an even more fervent prayer warrior during these seasons, because I usually insist he join me as I skip down the aisles of Target and Office Depot. It's further proof of how much my guy loves me.

We also have color-coded calendars on our phones that are synced with our children's devices. It feels like we live and die by these calendars.

"Mom, can I go here with so-and-so on Friday?" one child will ask.

"What's on the calendar?" is the typical response.

When I was a young mom, my days were dictated by feeding and sleep schedules. These days, our family calendar is filled months in advance with dance practices, performances, field trips, Travis Bird's business trips, orthodontist appointments, writing deadlines, family commitments, and the list goes on. It's insane. I just finished typing that list knowing full well how much more is on our plate, so to speak, and I want you to hear me.

I struggle with seamlessly fitting prayer into my life every single day. Yes, I pray, and I pray often. But my life is messy, and often I feel like this messiness bleeds into my coveted time with God. Yet I am so guilty of keeping that rhythm-of-rush pace. Even last night, I had difficulty going to sleep, because I was feeling the pressure of all that needs to be done.

If you're like me, you can relate to the Martha we meet in the Gospels of Luke and John. Her sister Mary and brother Lazarus (whom Jesus raised from the dead in John 11:1–44) are also present in Scripture. Jesus was quite familiar with the family, and John 11:5 tells us he loved them dearly. However, it's the story of Martha in the Gospel of Luke that makes me want to rethink my color-coded calendars.

> As Jesus and the disciples continued on their way to Jerusalem, they came to a certain village where a woman named Martha welcomed him into her home. Her sister, Mary, sat at the Lord's feet, listening to what he taught. But Martha was distracted by

> the big dinner she was preparing. She came to Jesus and said, "Lord, doesn't it seem unfair to you that my sister just sits here while I do all the work? Tell her to come and help me."
>
> But the Lord said to her, "My dear Martha, you are worried and upset over all these details! There is only one thing worth being concerned about. Mary has discovered it, and it will not be taken away from her." (Luke 10:38–42)

Can't you just picture Martha? Jesus was *literally* in her house. The Prince of Heaven was sitting in her living room. I vacuum before my bug lady comes to the house. Can you imagine the cleaning frenzy that would ensue if the Son of God were popping by for a visit? Honestly, I get Martha, and I see her as more than just a grouchy hostess.

As a Southern girl, hospitality ain't no joke. Southerners take pride and go to great lengths to make our guests feel welcome and loved. In Biblical times, the customs of hospitality were deeply imbedded in culture. Travelers were often vulnerable to the harsh arid conditions, and a hospitable offering of food and water could literally have meant the difference between life and death. In those times, a host was obliged to provide the traveler with food, water, and shelter. Abraham welcomed three such strangers into his tent in the Old Testament (Gen. 18:1–8). Scripture tells us that he eagerly ran to meet them and lavishly welcomed them. Abraham's words and actions, including bowing to the ground, may seem a little over the top by today's standards, but that was common practice for people of the ancient world.

Even though Martha knew Jesus well, he was still a guest in her home. The passage in Luke 10 oozes with Martha's anxiety. There's dinner to be made. Do we have everything we need, and will there be enough? The house is a wreck. Seriously, stuff is strewn everywhere. Does no one else bother to pick up his or her things? Who will help her clean? And because Martha is the one worried about dinner and cleaning, we can imagine she probably didn't have time to change into clean clothes and fix her face and hair. She was vibrating with feelings of, "Why isn't anyone else helping?"

Then there's her sister, Mary, just sitting calmly and peacefully at the feet of Jesus. While Martha stands sweating from her efforts, there is sweet

Mary, sitting without a care in the world. Can Mary not see the dirt on the floor and that the table still needs to be set? Martha is ready to jerk her sister up by her hair. We can tell Martha has had more than she can stand when she implores Jesus to make Mary get up and help her. Haven't you ever felt that deep frustration when you feel like all that needs to be done rests firmly upon your shoulders alone?

But what does Jesus say? He says, "Martha, dear Martha, you're fussing far too much and getting yourself worked up over nothing. One thing only is essential, and Mary has chosen it—it's the main course, and won't be taken from her" (Luke 10:41–42 MSG).

Can you imagine Jesus's calm and tender voice responding to the anxiousness he hears in Martha's voice? When someone asks you to bring it down a notch, it usually does nothing to ease the anxiety you may be feeling. Hearing someone tell me to chill out typically has the opposite effect and sets loose my inner Ouiser Boudreaux. You may remember Shirley MacLaine's character from the movie *Steel Magnolias*. She was ornery and filled to the brim with sass, perhaps responding to the suggestion of calming down with, "Oh no, they did *not*." But this is Jesus talking to Martha, his love for her beyond anything she could humanly comprehend. His love and calmness was likely evident in his tender tone as he spoke to Martha. Can you imagine?

"It's OK, dear Martha. *You* are OK. So many things weigh down your heart, and these details feel oh so important. Yet they are not. Only one thing is needed, and coming to me is the perfect thing to do.

"You came to me asking for help, and I want to lighten your load. I can carry the burden when you set those worries and concerns at my feet. You are released from preparing the perfect dinner, from having the perfectly cleaned home that is decorated just so, from being the perfect hostess, from having the perfectly coiffed hair. All of those things are fleeting, but my love for you is not. The things of this world are nothing compared to the life I have prepared for you."

That is the sweet, sweet assurance we need in the midst of a culture that encourages us to fill our calendars to the brim, to be part of everything for fear of missing anything. These are more lies the enemy feeds us to keep us from what our hearts truly crave and need—communion with God.

I love that Martha came to Jesus in the midst of her struggle. Prayer doesn't have to look like stopping and secluding yourself from the world. I want to encourage you to embrace prayer as a natural act of worship that fits seamlessly into your day, not a color-coded "to do" on your calendar.

CONFESSIONS OF A BUSY, DISTRACTED PRAY-ER

by Katie M. Reid

Designed to be a doer, like Martha from the Bible, I am more apt to make lists of what I learn *about* God and more inclined to do things *for* God than I am to spend hours in my prayer closet calling out *to* God. Who am I kidding? My closet lacks room for prayer, too. But, man, I like checking things off my to-do list, prayer included.

As a busy mom of five, my prayers are more like SOS flares when I'm stressed, or quick declarations of God's majesty as I point out his handiwork to my kids while driving down country roads in our rusty minivan. As a firstborn overachiever, my lackluster prayer life feels like a bad mark on my imaginary spiritual report card.

But I've missed the mark with this line of thinking, haven't I?

Prayer is not a have-to; it's a get-to. It is simpler and more sacred than we realize. It's not up to us alone to get it right or get it done. God is ready and able to help us in our weakness; our part is to ask him for help and to participate in the process. I put so much pressure on myself to perfect prayer that I miss the beauty of it: an open conversation with my Lord and free access to the One who sits on the throne and resides in the home of my heart.

As a list maker, I find comfort in scripted prayers. Not because I have nothing original to say, but because that kind of prayer provides a clear focus for what to pray, or at least how to get started. For example, in Stormie Omartian's book *The Power of a Praying Wife*, I can turn to the chapter about a husband's health and pray that scripted prayer on behalf of my man.

Sometimes I write out my prayers in a journal because when I just think them, my mind wanders (or runs) to my ever-growing to-do list. Tethering my thoughts through writing keeps me alert as I pray. Through journaling, I can revisit these prayers and record when and how God answered. Another tool that helps this modern Martha pray is to make a list of what I learn about God, Jesus, and the Holy Spirit as I read the Bible. As I come across verses that reveal characteristics about each member of the Trinity, I turn those character qualities into a prayer.

Let me give you an example from John 14:16–17 (ESV).

1. Read the passage.

   16 And I will ask the Father, and he will give you another Helper, to be with you forever, 17 even the Spirit of truth, whom the world cannot receive, because it neither sees him nor knows him. You know him, for he dwells with you and will be in you.

2. Based on what you read, make a list of what you learned. Record the reference next to your findings, so you can easily access it later.

   John 14:16—**The Father**, gives us a **Helper** (to be with us forever).
   John 14:17—**The Spirit of truth** . . . we can know him . . . he dwells with you and is in you.

3. Turn your findings into a prayer.

   Thank you, God, that you are my Father and that you provide a Helper to be with me forever. Thank you, Spirit of truth, for allowing me to know you. I am so grateful that you dwell with me and live within me. What a gift you are from the Father. Amen.

Realizing that prayer is honest communication with God—not a performance—can make a big difference. It's like the texts I send to my husband throughout the day—sometimes they are quick and to the point, other times they express affection, sometimes they are peppered with questions, and other times they are full of thanksgiving. As worship leader and songwriter Steffany Getzinger recently said, "My prayer life now looks like an open conversation and not just a closed door."[2]

Realizing that prayer has many expressions is freeing. Prayer can be an ongoing dialogue, a cry, an SOS signal flare, a recognition of majesty, a quiet moment, an extended time of reflection, an expression of affection, a peppering of questions, and a communication of thanks. Steffany Gretzinger also said, "It's all about our awareness. We're always connected to God. We cannot escape him. He's in every fiber of our being."[3] Prayer is connecting with the One who runs the universe yet is closer than your next breath—both powerful and personal.

Ask God to guide you when you fear you're failing at this whole prayer thing. Trust him to provide a framework for your wandering heart—not to lock you in but to release you into a spacious place, where you remember who he is and who you are in his heart: accepted, beloved, cared for. Prayer is not a punishment; it's a practice that ushers in the peace that is already yours in Christ.

Give these different frameworks a try: the Lord's Prayer, scripted prayer, journaling your prayers, praying the characteristics of God, and text-style prayers. (Don't we wish we had God's phone number? Ha!)

EVERYONE CAN USE A LITTLE GRACE

This chapter has been about providing a framework for prayer. The Lord's Prayer provides a beautiful template for us to personalize. Next is another tool to use as you become more creative with your exploration of prayer. In a journal or on a piece of paper, write the word *grace* vertically. Then use each letter to stand for an action in your prayer. You can be as concise or as verbose as you like. For example:

G = **Gratitude**
Begin your prayer with praise and thanksgiving.

R = **Repent**
Confess your sins and seek forgiveness.

A = **Ask**
Lay your petitions and earnest requests at God's feet.

C = **Consider**
Take a moment to reflect what the Holy Spirit may be saying.

E = **Esteem**
End with praise and worship.

For those friends looking for a little more direction on how to structure their prayers, this is just another tool to add to your toolbox. Use it daily or as the mood strikes. You can write these prayers down or simply pray them from your heart. God receives them all.

Sandy Says

"Grace stands for God's Riches at Christ's Expense."

> Be prepared. You're up against far more than you can handle on your own. Take all the help you can get, every weapon God has issued, so that when it's all over but the shouting, you'll still be on your feet. Truth, righteousness, peace, faith, and salvation are more than words. Learn how to apply them. You'll need them throughout your life. God's Word is an indispensable weapon. In the same way, prayer is essential in this ongoing warfare. Pray hard and long. Pray for your brothers and sisters. Keep your eyes open. Keep each other's spirits up so that no one falls behind or drops out. (Eph. 6:13–18 MSG)

our Father
in heaven,
hallowed be your Name,
your KINGDOM come,
your will be done, on earth as in heaven.
GIVE US today our daily bread.
FORGIVE US our sins as we
forgive those who sin against us.
SAVE US from the time of trial,
and DELIVER US from evil.
For the KINGDOM
the POWER and the GLORY
are yours,
now and
FOREVER
AMEN

Dear Lord,

Help us realize that our never-ending lists of to-dos are inconsequential compared to my time with you. Help each of us to seek you first in all things and trust your plan instead of ours. Give us release from the highlighted lists and color-coded calendars, Father. Ignite in our spirits a deeper love that passes all understanding, and put a fire in our bellies that can only be quenched by spending time with you. Thank you, God, for loving us so much that you sent your one and only Son to pay the blood price for our sins. We can't even begin to fathom that kind of love, Lord, but we are thankful nonetheless and gratefully reach for your gift of unending grace. We love you, Father.

In Jesus's precious name,

Amen

CHAPTER SIX

CREATIVE BIBLE JOURNALING

When my girls were entering the second and fifth grades, we embarked on what would become known as "the great homeschool experiment." Emma Kathryn was still young enough that her perception of school with mommy sounded fun and exciting. However, Ashley was acutely aware that her mama was not a schoolteacher and had a pretty serious adverse reaction to most math homework. I think she was as nervous as I was.

Of course, I'd researched the perfect curriculum for us and planned our entire year (in my aesthetically pleasing planner, of course). Truthfully, too, the homeschool memes of Ryan Gosling were pretty inspiring. Even now, when Travis Bird wants to make me laugh, he walks by and says, "Hey, girl. Want to go to dinner and talk about classical education?" Anyway, I digress . . .

On the first day of homeschool, I don't know who was more anxious, Ashley or me. Travis Bird was so sweet and hesitant as he left for work that day. He said I looked completely terrified. I was clearly overwhelmed and worried I had bitten off more than I could chew. By lunch on that first day, I was exhausted. I had no idea what I was doing, and by midday, I knew my children were definitely not going to be any smarter after spending a year at home with me. I wasn't even through the first day, and I felt like a complete failure.

After lunch, I remember telling the girls we were going to spend time reading our Bibles together. We needed a break from everything else. Honestly, they looked relieved. Now this was something their mom could do. We opened our Bibles at the very beginning and began to read aloud. Then I gave my girls a set of colored pencils and a journal and asked them to describe what the Scripture passage meant to them. They eagerly opened their journals and began to color and draw.

I was totally fine with this. I've colored for years, friends. *Years.* Just like Barbara Mandrell said she was country when country wasn't cool. Well, I was coloring long before adult coloring was cool. While my friends in college were receiving fun care packages of snacks and trendy magazines, mine were full of *Precious Moments* and *Strawberry Shortcake* coloring books. The struggle was real.

CREATIVITY IN THE PAGES OF THE BIBLE

I thought about how coloring and drawing might translate to prayer. I loved the idea of taking colors to Scripture and inviting the Holy Spirit to work in my heart as I contemplated the words I'd read.

Creativity is innately woven into God's character. To see the marvelous wonders and works of his hands makes him more evident to us. The beautiful sunset over the horizon, the symphony of sounds we hear throughout nature, the majestic mountains and seascapes, even the sounds and views from your own backyard—these are all echoes of God's splendor and evidence of his creativity. In fact, the Master Artist's first recorded activity reflected his creative nature (Gen. 1:1). As his image bearers, we share creative characteristics, too. Just because you may not be able to draw a straight line or design a piece of art on your own does not mean you lack artistry.

Creativity is expressed in a multitude of ways: song, dance, art, architecture, writing, battle tactics, and so on. We find plenty of examples within the pages of Scripture.

CREATIVITY THROUGH WISDOM

Solomon was the third king of Israel (965–926 BC) and the last king of the united kingdom of Israel and Judah. He could have asked God for anything, but he requested wisdom to govern God's people (1 Kings 3:9). Besides Jesus, Solomon was the wisest man ever to live. Because Solomon expressed wisdom creatively, his beautiful words captivated generations of people long after his time on earth was done.

We need only look to the books of Proverbs, Lamentations, Song of Solomon, and Ecclesiastes for plentiful examples of his creative expressions. Solomon proved wisdom yields creativity, as his creative nature was expressed through three thousand proverbs and more than a thousand songs (1 Kings 4:32).

CREATIVITY THROUGH SERVING

Tabitha (translated in Greek as Dorcas), from the town of Joppa and whom Peter raised from the dead, earned a reputation among her people as a generous seamstress (Acts 9:36–41). She was well-known in her village for using her creative sewing skills to bless less fortunate women. When Tabitha fell ill and died, many of those she had helped gathered near her body to mourn. In fact, when Peter arrived at the house where Tabitha's body lay, Acts tells us "the room was filled with widows who were weeping and showing him the coats and other clothes Dorcas had made for them" (Acts 9:39). She used her God-given, creative gift to serve others.

CREATIVITY THROUGH POETRY AND MUSIC

The great King David, a man after God's own heart (Acts 13:22), displayed his creativity through his love of poetry, song, and dance. This is the same David who defeated Goliath! David was well-known as a fierce warrior and mighty king, and the nation of Israel prospered under his rule. Yet his last words on earth reflected his creative nature and were offered to God as an act of worship. "Here are the last words of David, son of Jesse: the words of the one raised up, the anointed one of Jacob's True God, the sweet songwriter of Israel. David: The Spirit of the Eternal speaks through me; His voice emerges from my mouth" (2 Sam. 23:1–2 Voice).

CREATIVITY THROUGH TEACHING

Jesus expressed spiritual truths from everyday life and creatively explained them through his teaching of parables. He often used ordinary, everyday objects to teach those around him about God. When Jesus was near a well, he used water (John 4:4–42). When he sat in a boat by the sea, Jesus said the kingdom was like a fishing net (Matt. 13:47–50). He told the people to consider the lilies (Luke 12:27–28), the sparrows, and the hairs on their heads (Matt. 10:29–31). Jesus referred to a fig tree (Luke 13:6–9), a mustard seed (Matt. 17:20), salt (Matt. 5:13–16), and many other common items from everyday life that the people he was teaching would understand.

The expression of creativity is multifaceted and provides ample opportunity to explore worship with God in a variety of ways. That's not to say there isn't much to learn and love through traditional methods of prayer, because there is. I'm simply inviting you as a child of the heavenly king, who shares the creative traits of our Father, to explore other creative ways to commune with God, and one of those ways is through Bible journaling.

When I handed my girls the colored pencils and a journal on that first day of homeschool, their eyes were opened to a new way for them to fellowship with God. We may have struggled through the rest of our schoolwork that first year, but Bible time was something we all looked forward to experiencing each day. Even now, I sometimes find them in their rooms alone, Bibles open with journals and colored pencils close by.

Their Bible journaling is a form of prayer, because they use these moments to communicate reflections of their hearts with the God who created them. It's beautiful and deeply personal.

SO WHAT IS BIBLE JOURNALING?

By now, you have likely heard of Bible journaling, which is simply a creative way to engage with Scripture. It can transform the way you spend time in the Word, offering a fresh approach to your regular prayer time. Prayer is absolutely an act of worship, and using a method like Bible journaling enables us to incorporate creative worship into our quiet time with

God. Some people draw in the margins of their Bibles, doodling as they meditate on what they've read.

I personally enjoy Bible journaling in three different ways. Sometimes I create my own illustrations when I'm inspired and time allows. Other times, I might color in a Bible that includes pre-drawn art in the margins. This saves time, but it also allows me the creative outlet I usually crave. The *Beautiful Word Bible* is a great example, but there are plenty of journaling Bible options in the marketplace. The third way I sometimes journal in my Bible may make you laugh and roll your eyes, but it's true. Sometimes I use my Bible journaling time to diagram Scriptures in the margin of my Bible.

I know, I know. It's not for everyone, but as a writer, this type of journaling really speaks to my spirit. Thinking about each role every word plays in the sentence really helps me meditate on the Scripture I've read or underlined, and it inevitably leaves me hungry for more of God's Word. The Holy Spirit speaks to each of us in the way each of us will best hear him. You do you, friend. What works for me may not resonate with your spirit in the same way. You have to find the types of prayers that feed your spirit, and Bible journaling is just one of many creative prayer outlets you can explore.

The best part of exploring this creative prayer method is this: it doesn't require a skilled artist. I have no doubt my second grader's Bible journaling entries were just as beautiful to God as the most intricately crafted design of a professional artist. All that matters is that you're willing to experience God and his Word in a creative and personal way.

There are plenty of sites that provide extensive supply lists and tutorials for getting started in Bible journaling. Check the Resources section at the end of the book for a few of my favorite Bible journaling resources. The purpose of Part Two in this book is to get you thinking about new creative methods of prayer, encourage you to try a few of them, and walk you through how to get started.

I started Bible journaling with a journal-style Bible, a set of colored pencils, and my favorite Tombow dual brush pens. Included in this chapter is a traceable art page for practice, and there is more inspiration to be found in the Creative Contemplation Extras section in Part Three.

BEGIN WITH FRIENDSHIP

In the Bible, Abraham is the only person in the Old Testament who is called the friend of God (2 Chron. 20:7; James 2:23). We know from Scripture that Abraham had many encounters with God throughout his journey to the Promised Land. One of these encounters was God testing Abraham's faith when he asked Abraham to sacrifice his one and only son, Isaac (Gen. 22). Perhaps this was a foreshadowing of what God was willing to do for all of us. "For God so loved the world that he gave his one and only Son" (John 3:16 NIV).

Could it be that Abraham understood God's heart? Through that willingness to sacrifice his greatest treasure, Abraham may have had a glimpse into what God was willing to do for the sake of all mankind. Regardless, Scripture makes it clear that God loved Abraham and considered him a friend (Isa. 41:8).

Can you imagine? *A friend of God.*

Look back at the lyrics to "What a Friend We Have in Jesus" in Chapter Two. This hymn was written as a poem by a man named Joseph Scriven, an Irish immigrant who moved to Canada from Ireland in the mid-1800s. Twice he was engaged to be married, and each time his intended died before their wedding day. Joseph spent most of his life working among impoverished widows and the ailing. It was reported that he even shared his own clothes with those less fortunate.

One day, Joseph fell ill, and a friend who had come to visit found the poem by his bedside. Joseph reportedly told his friend, "The Lord and I did it between us."[1] He never intended for anyone to see it. Charles Converse was Joseph's friend and attorney, and upon Joseph's death, Charles set the poem to music, which became the well-loved hymn we know today.

Look at the lyrics again. Despite the thorns and storms Joseph endured, he continued to seek a relationship with God. In all seasons, through all trials, he held out his hand to Yahweh.

Sandy Says

"What a concept that we choose to be thankful in all circumstances. Every circumstance gives us the choice to draw near him—whether it is good or bad—always thanking him for the opportunity to trust him and be excited what God is going to do."

CRAVING A DEEPER RELATIONSHIP WITH GOD

by Ashley Bird

My freshman year of high school, I started a new school. While I didn't know many of the students, there were a few people who reached out and helped me with the transition. One of these welcoming new friends was a boy in my Latin class. His name was Adam, and he instantly drew me in with his warmth. Our Latin class was a small, ragtag group of students who bonded over study sessions we were required to attend before school even began.

Adam was one of just a handful of students I knew on that first day at a new school. As the first few months of school passed, we quickly became friends. I loved being around Adam, because he always radiated such joy and positivity. There was never a dull moment with him, and he never failed to make others laugh and smile.

This is why the news that Adam had taken his life came as such a devastating shock to everyone who knew and loved him. I still remember the moment my parents told me. At first, I couldn't understand his actions or why God had let him take his life. Adam was so loved!

He brought much joy to those around him. I was confused, sad, and angry. So many tears. My parents listened when I needed to process my feelings and offered me no small amount of comforting words.

The truth was that Adam's death rocked everyone who knew him to the core. After many heart-to-heart conversations with God and my parents, I've come to realize I may not ever understand Adam's choice to end his life, but I have confidence he no longer questions how much he is loved. The minute he met Jesus, Adam was enveloped with the love and peace that passes all of our human understanding.

After Adam's death, I turned to Bible journaling for consolation. I've used this method of prayer off and on since my mom introduced it to my sister and me a few years ago. It's a simple and effective way for me to talk with God. When I first began Bible journaling, I talked quite a bit to God, but even more so after Adam's death. I spoke to God as if he were my best friend, because he does know me better than anyone else, even my parents.

Part of the process of Bible journaling for me was learning that when my mouth is closed and my heart and ears are open, God's voice can be heard more clearly. I practice this best when I'm doodling and thinking about a Scripture I've read. For a while after Adam's funeral, I distanced myself from the world around me and just listened for God's voice. I was so eager to hear him. I spent hours drawing, coloring, and listening. By practicing being quiet in this way, I was able to explore a new part of my relationship with the Lord. He was so faithful to use my grief in a positive way.

Growing up, my parents have always taught me that God wastes nothing. They say every experience—even the worst imaginable—can be used by God for something amazing. I'm learning some circumstances of life will be difficult, but I'm also learning to trust God to use these experiences in a way that will shape me into the person he has designed me to be. After losing Adam, I found this truth difficult to believe for a bit. I was angry at God. Through my Bible journaling, though, I sought more of his truth instead of turning my back on him.

If anything, I want to know more of God's truth, not less. I crave a deep and genuine relationship with him.

Creativity comes in many forms, and Bible journaling is a fun and easy method of prayer for anyone to explore. So no worries if you're not an artist or anything like that. I think God loves the outcome of Bible journaling regardless of the skill. I know I do, too.

CREATIVE CONTEMPLATION

Let's walk through a few easy steps to guide you on your Bible journaling journey.

STEP 1

Read and reflect on a passage from Scripture. Because we've been talking so much about what prayer means and being a friend to Jesus, let's start here.

> "Then Jesus said, 'Come to me,
> all of you who are weary and carry heavy burdens,
> and I will give you rest.'"
> —Matthew 11:28

STEP 2

Pick out key words in the verse that stand out to you. For example: "Come," "weary," "burdens," and "rest." Remember to pick out whatever words stand out to *you*. Don't overthink this. It's like brainstorming. There's no judgment in the brainstorming circle. Just write on a piece of paper the words from the passage that are speaking to your spirit. And if the Spirit so leads you, maybe you should try your hand at diagramming!

STEP 3

Now, how do you visualize these words? Don't be shy about looking on Instagram and Pinterest for inspiration. @fischtales and @rebekahrjones are two of my favorites. As you research, you will discover vastly creative people who make amazing, beautiful Bible journaling pages. Do *not* be intimidated by their masterpieces!

Bible journaling is about *your* personal prayer time with God. Your efforts will be just as staggeringly wondrous in the eyes of God as the most precious works of art, because it's *your* offering of worship to him. The goal is fellowship and friendship, not perfection.

Think about a visual representation of what the words you wrote down might look like to you, and sketch them in your journal or on another sheet of paper.

STEP 4

Now add color! Grab your colored pencils, markers, or crayons and go over your sketch. Then fill it in with more doodles and color.

A WORD TO THE WISE

Yes, Bible journaling is all the rage, but it's important not to lose sight of the purpose behind this creative method of prayer. It's just that: a prayer, your personal act of worship to God, a time of fellowship between you and Jesus. One of the pitfalls of Bible journaling is overcomplicating it. If you feel overwhelmed, take a breath and simplify. Don't feel like you need to finish your Bible journaling entry in one sitting, either. Some entries in my Bible took several days, and sometimes the Spirit urges me to spend more time with a particular passage of Scripture.

What I love about Bible journaling is that it puts our God-given creativity to use and keeps us in the Word. As Christians, the sword of the Spirit is vital in our battle against the enemy. It's the only offensive piece of armor that we carry (Eph. 6:10–20). Every other piece of the armor of God defends against the enemy's attacks. Immersing ourselves in the Word of God is not only essential; it is critical as we fight against an enemy who is relentless in his pursuit of us and ours.

We are also undeniably living in a selfie world and the age of social media. Bible journaling is a great tool in these outlets, because it's shareable. As Christians, our top two priorities are to know God and to help make him known (Matt. 22:37–40). Sharing your Bible journaling entries is completely optional, and there's no judgment for keeping those special works between you and God. However, if you feel so led, share your images through social media. God can use these outlets in a positive way, and you might be surprised at the depth and breadth of impact your Bible journaling entries have on others. As George Müller said,

> I saw more clearly than ever, that the first great and primary business to which I ought to attend every day was, to have my soul happy in the Lord. The first thing to be concerned about was not, how I might serve the Lord, how I might glorify the Lord; but how I might get my soul into a happy state, and how my inner man may be nourished. . . . I saw that the most important thing I had to do was to give myself to the reading of the Word of God and to meditation of it.[2]

I've included another Bible journaling practice prompt for you to trace or color. Add doodles of your own, or simply grab your favorite colored pencils and add your personal flair to the drawing provided for you.

As you explore and dabble in this creative method of prayer, please share with me! I would love to see and celebrate some of your beautiful offerings of Bible journaling prayers. Remember that your artwork and your words are just as lovely to God as the most world-renowned artists and craftsmen. I pray this creative method of prayer inspires you and draws you nearer to Jesus. The goal is always to know him deeper. Go forth and color!

Father God,

Thank you for the gift of creativity. The abundance of your artistry is apparent all around us, and we are in awe of you. Lord, please bless this time of fellowship as the reader explores a new way to fellowship with you and meditate on your Word. Quiet her mind and any distractions so that she may see nothing but you. Impart your wisdom and help her to remember that she is yours, and nothing can separate her from you.

In Jesus's name,

Amen

WHAT
A
FRIEND
WE
HAVE
in
JESUS

CHAPTER SEVEN

CREATIVE NATURE WALK PRAYER

After my second daughter was born, my body was a wreck. I'd gained approximately seventy-five pounds, never feeling well enough during my pregnancy to exercise. I was on and off bed rest for months, and then she was born nearly six weeks prematurely. If you've seen the movie *Ghostbusters* (1984) with Dan Aykroyd and Bill Murray, you may be familiar with the Stay Puft Marshmallow Man who attacked the Ghostbusters at the end of the film. We joked that by the time my baby girl made her debut, I looked like the Stay Puft Marshmallow Girl, and that probably wasn't far off the mark. It felt like every inch of my body was retaining water in some way. My husband and I even made it a game to see how long an indentation would last after pressing a finger into my arm or leg. I know. That's sad. Sometimes it's the little things, people.

The day after I was cleared by my doctor to begin exercising, we joined the YMCA. I faithfully went to the gym every single day and walked on the treadmill or walked around my neighborhood. I even tried the group fitness classes. At first, I could only make it through the Silver Sneakers yoga class. Seriously, I was the youngest participant *by far*, and many of those sweet ladies were way more flexible. I stuck with it, though, and the pounds began to come off. The more weight I lost, the more energy I felt. This was a good thing, since my baby girl was still not sleeping through the night. Eventually, I added Pilates and hot yoga to my workout regimen. Before long, my bloodwork was normal again, and I was gaining the strength and flexibility reminiscent of my days as a dancer.

My BFF and I even joined Weight Watchers together. Oh, friends. She and I had been pregnant at the same time, her son born just three months before my daughter. When it came to lunch, we were pregnant women on a mission. I don't know how many days we arrived at Luby's right when they opened, eagerly waiting in line for our LuAnn plates. Come to think of it, that might be where I first met some of my friends in the Silver Sneakers class.

We were committed to getting healthy after our pregnancies. Each week, my best gal pal and I donned the most lightweight clothing we owned for weigh-in at our local Weight Watchers office. Afterward, we skipped to the nearest Freebird's for our celebratory "yay, we're losing weight" burrito. Some weeks, we had setbacks. However, for the most part, we stuck to the plan, worked out, and encouraged one another to stay the course. After months of determination, we both met our weight goals. It felt so great.

At that time, I was running almost six miles at a time, three times a week—the most I'd ever run at once—*ever*. I wouldn't say at that point that I *loved* running, but I no longer hated it. I could get through the distance I was running without feeling like I was about to die. To me, that was a win. But one day, like Forrest Gump, I stopped mid-run. I decided I didn't want to run anymore. Y'all, this really happened. Halfway through my route, I turned around and walked home. It was like I had completed an important quest, and my work was done. I kept up with my walking and hot yoga, but as far as running, I thought Proverbs 28:1 might be on to something. No offense to my runner friends . . . "The wicked run away when no one is chasing them."

AN ATTITUDE OF WORSHIP

Earlier in this book, I talked about being so tired in those early days of motherhood that I simply held my Bible in my hands, because I was too weary to read. The only quiet time I had during that season was when I was walking alone. Sometimes I listened to music, but often I walked and absorbed the sounds of nature around me. It was in those quiet moments that I felt most in tune with the Holy Spirit, and I began to use this time to pray.

I love my family dearly, but my home is rife with distractions—even now. When my babies were younger, this was more so. Don't get me wrong, friends. One day, my house will be spotless and silent. I know I'll long for the days of LEGO land mines and the copious amounts of laundry my children currently generate each day.

Yet even in this busy season of marriage and parenthood, I see glimpses of God's blessings stamped all over the beautifully imperfect life he's given me. Just a few minutes ago, I popped my head into my oldest daughter's room. She and her sister were sitting on the floor, and my oldest daughter was teaching her younger sister how to braid her own hair. They were giggling and enjoying an ordinary, everyday moment together. I embrace these breathtakingly wonderful "God winks" and try to remember to pause when they happen to say, "Thank you, Father."

However, when I am walking, that is a quiet time when I'm able to be more intentional about my conversation with God. My attitude is one of worship, a focused time where I've pressed pause on my crazy life to shift my gaze solely to my heavenly Father. I wish I could say I exude an attitude of worship in every moment of every day, but that's simply not true—especially during college football season. What can I say? I'm a messy work in progress. This is just another of the many reasons I need Jesus.

DISCIPLINE OF SPIRITUAL TRAINING

Let's talk for a minute about what *discipline* means, because sometimes this word holds a negative connotation and is associated with punishment. Discipline comes from *disciplina*, the Latin word for teaching or instruction, but *disciplina* is derived from the Latin word *discipulus*, which gives us the English word *disciple*. What were Jesus's followers called in ancient times and still known as today? That's right, friends. *Disciples*.

As Christians, our faith requires a commitment to personal discipline like that of an athlete. Paul compares physical training with spiritual training in his letter to the Corinthians.

> You've all been to the stadium and seen the athletes race. Everyone runs; one wins. Run to win. All good athletes train hard. They do it for a gold medal that tarnishes and fades. You're after one that's gold eternally. I don't know about you, but I'm running hard for the finish line. I'm giving it everything I've got. No sloppy living for me! I'm staying alert and in top condition. I'm not going to get caught napping, telling everyone else all about it and then missing out myself. (1 Cor. 9:24–27 MSG)

I love this comparison from Paul. As a dancer for more than twenty years, I spent countless hours pushing myself physically and mentally to be the very best I could be. Sometimes I fell. I experienced injuries and had to sit out performances. Yet I still persevered. None of these things kept me from training and pursuing my best physical self. I did this because I *loved* to dance.

In Psalm 50:17, God says to the wicked, "You hate discipline, and you cast my words behind your back" (NIV). The true disciples of Jesus practiced discipline not because they were afraid of punishment, but because they *loved* Jesus. As I accept the need for discipline in my life as a follower of Jesus, I do so because I love him and want a deeper relationship with him.

Can you imagine if we took the intense determination that athletes use for training and applied it to our spiritual lives? 1 Timothy 4:7–8 says, "Reject worldly fables. Refuse old wives' tales. Instead, train yourself toward godliness. Although training your body has certain payoffs, godliness benefits all things—holding promise for life here and now and promise for the life that is coming" (VOICE).

Your soul is your spiritual center. Like other aspects of the human body, the spirit needs to be exercised like a muscle. Without intentional effort to move and exercise our earthly bodies, we become encased in layers of flab (or, as I like to call it, fluff); we find ourselves winded from light activity and lose overall physical strength. In the same way, ignoring our soul's training leads to the accumulation of spiritual "fluff." Our moral muscles atrophy, losing much-needed tone and strength. When that happens, we become more susceptible to the ways of the world.

Nutrition plays an important part in our physical and spiritual health as well. What we feed our body influences how our body performs. Likewise, what we feed our spirit influences how our soul performs. If we fuel our bodies with nothing but junk food, they won't work as efficiently as they would if we were to fuel them with healthy food choices. Most athletes are very particular about what they put into their bodies. Similarly, if we fill our minds with unhealthy thoughts and images, our souls reflect what we've allowed inside. Like Paul says, we need to be spiritually disciplined to finish our race and claim the prize of eternity with Jesus.

So what does spiritual discipline look like? Well, it does *not* look like punishment, friends. My mind drifts to my mom, who until the time she could no longer write on her own, spent every night before bed reading the Word of God and writing in her Bible. My mother had physical limitations my entire life, but she never allowed those obstacles to keep her from sprinting toward the eternal finish line. She wrote in her Bible every night, not just for herself, but for her loved ones as well. We are still benefitting from her discipline as she left those prayers and words of wisdom for us to find. You're glimpsing what that looks like in the "Sandy says" sections of each chapter. Spiritual discipline looks like being in the Word of God regularly (Job 23:12). Yet my mom didn't continue this practice so diligently because she was afraid of the consequences if she didn't. She spent time in God's Word every night because she loved Jesus so deeply and wanted to know him better.

Discipline requires self-control, which you'll remember is one of the fruits of the Spirit. Discipline looks like flexing our spiritual muscles and asking the Holy Spirit to cultivate the fruits of the Spirit within us: love, joy, peace, patience, kindness, goodness, faithfulness, gentleness, and self-control (Gal. 5:22–23). This cluster of fruit should be reflected in the actions of every Christian—that's our aspiration as followers of Christ. We know from Chapter Three that prayers for the fruit of the Spirit are often answered in the form of opportunities to practice them, which is also opportunity to stretch your spiritual muscles.

Spiritual discipline may also look like spending time in prayer. Remember, the more you time you spend with Jesus, the more your relationship grows. Spiritual discipline looks like spending time listening to the Word of God proclaimed by others, perhaps in church by your pastor or another Christian leader (Luke 5:1; Rom. 10:17). It looks like spending time with like-minded Christians who affirm one another in faith and encourage one another to stay the course, keeping our eyes on the eternal prize (Prov. 12:26; Prov. 27:17). It looks like worshipping in song as King David did. It looks like pressing pause on our busy lives to observe God's goodness around us and offer thanks for his faithfulness.

It isn't realistic to be completely submerged in circles with Christians who believe exactly as we do. However, a community that supports our beliefs, encourages us to search, and worships and prays with us is so important in our growth. Furthermore, believers who don't agree with us help us go deeper in our search for truth. Making the name of Jesus known and spreading the Good News is done most effectively when we ourselves are strong in the Word. This requires diligence on our part to train our spiritual muscles for strength and endurance.

When I was a dancer, I had a goal in mind, ambitiously striving to achieve the objective I'd set for myself. As Christians, we have a goal, too, and that is to spend eternity with our Lord and Savior, Jesus Christ. There is a longing in our souls that only God can satisfy. No earthly pleasure or activity can fill this space, and God designed us this way on purpose.

Take a moment with me and ask God to give us a heart for discipleship, the hunger and passion needed for our spiritual training, and the will to run our spiritual race with strength and endurance. Read the following words aloud:

Lord,

Please give me the discipline to stretch and strengthen my spiritual muscles. Open the eyes of my heart, so I can see you. I desire you above all things, Lord. Help my words, my choices, and my actions to bear witness to your glory. El Shaddai, I love you and praise your holy name.

Amen

THE UNPREDICTABLE PATH OF FAITH

Life happens to all of us. Illness. Divorce. A new job. Injury. Relocating to a new place. Death of a loved one. An infinite number of *things* can knock us off our path of faith.

When my mom was alive, I talked with her every day, often more than once. When she fell ill, it rocked our world. We rallied. We prayed. We trusted. The last words she spoke to me were, "Hi, baby," whispered from her hospice bed less than a week before she died. In all the ways I've missed her presence, not hearing her voice has been the toughest. By far.

Yet, despite my mom's illness, the world kept right on turning. It moved so quickly around me, it left me feeling dizzy in my brokenness. Where was God in the shattered pieces of my family that were left behind after my mom was gone? I couldn't process what life was supposed to look like without her, but I made a valiant effort to go through the motions. I took children to school. I drove them to and from extracurricular activities. I worked. I attended church with my family. I smiled and tried to listen when others spoke to me. However, inside I felt so completely empty.

During those months my mom was ill, I didn't have time for regular workouts. When I could make time, I often walked at a park near our house where the trees drape like a canopy over the trail and a small stream runs parallel to the path. Those walks, which felt few and far between during that painful season, were like a lifeline to God. I played worship music as loud as my headphones would allow, breathed in the air around me, and took in the sights of nature and wildlife. Occasionally, I paused and stared as the water rushed over pebbles in the stream. I prayed for my mom, for healing, for strength, for courage to trust God's plan.

I'm not ashamed to say that my mom's illness rocked the foundation of my faith. I was angry, friends. I cried and ranted to God, asking over and over, "Why her?" Why *my* mom? We needed her. My daddy needed her.

My brothers needed her. Her grandchildren needed her. My girls needed her. *I* needed her. I even offered God other names to take instead of my mom. Seriously. In that broken place, I tried to barter with God.

It was in those quiet moments on these walks that I often had tears streaming down my face, when I allowed myself to embrace the helplessness I felt, when I finally surrendered control to God. It was on one of my walks with God when I finally accepted that he was going to heal my mom his way, not mine. He wanted to free my mom from her broken body that kept her from running like he longed for her to do. Her wounded earthly body was holding her spirit captive, and he longed to set her free.

Just like I imagined he once spoke to Martha in the way she needed to hear him, I heard Jesus whispering words of comfort and love to me.

"It's OK, dear Catherine. *You* are OK. So many things weigh on your heart, and these details feel oh so important. Yet they are not. Only one thing is needed, and coming to me is the perfect thing to do.

"You came to me asking for help, and I want to lighten your load. I can carry the burden when you set those worries and concerns at my feet. You are released from worrying over your mom, for she is mine as are you, from keeping the perfectly paced life in the midst of this painful storm, from being strong for all those around you. That is for me to do. Earthly pain and suffering is fleeting, but my love for you is not. The things of this world are nothing compared to the life I have prepared for you. Trust me, daughter."

Sandy Says

"It was in one of those *crying your eyes out until your mascara runs* moments that I heard God's tender voice ask, 'Who touched me?' It was I. He had heard. I had touched his heart. He had touched mine. During that moment of intimacy like never before, God showed me that what the world meant for bad, he was going to use for good."

I surrendered and finally prayed, "Your will be done, Lord, not mine." That didn't take away the pain of my mom's death, but I felt the Holy Spirit moving within me. I realized the truth that our God wastes nothing, and I trusted all the pain and suffering would be used for something amazing. As usual, God didn't disappoint.

For years, I've heard friends talk about when they came to faith, how they came to know Jesus. My husband can tell you the exact date he became a Christian. I always thought my story was nothing special. I grew up knowing faith was a treasure, a gift that meant we could spend eternity together with our Savior. I can't remember a time when I didn't talk to Jesus. My childhood memories are filled to the brim with attending church with my family, spending Friday nights singing songs of worship and praise in our living room, and watching my parents pray over others. My mom was a prayer warrior, my grandmother before her, and my great-grandmother before her. The legacy they left for me is one of faith, and I've come to realize that's undeniably special.

My mom lived her faith unapologetically loud and proud. Like Paul encourages us to do (1 Cor. 9:24–27), she ran at a full sprint toward the eternal finish line, leaving love notes for her loved ones along the way, encouraging us to stay the course of our own races. Just last weekend, my daddy and I were reading through my mom's Bible. We came across this handwritten note.

> September 9, 2016
> Today's diagnosis was not what we wanted to hear. Lord Jesus, please strengthen us and give us courage and faith to run the race. Praise to you and thank you for all you do! You are my strength, my salvation and Redeemer. Praising you tonight!

Even in the face of insurmountable mountains, my mom trusted and praised God. The psalmist says we are to enter the Lord's presence with thanksgiving (Ps. 100:1). When we exalt in our Lord and lift him up, Jesus is lifted up (John 12:32), and the enemy trembles at his name (James 2:19).

Well done, Mom. Your race has been won, and now we "look to those in heaven and carry on their legacy of faith." According to J. I. Packer:

> God uses chronic pain and weakness, along with other afflictions, as his chisel for sculpting our lives. Felt weakness deepens dependence on Christ for strength each day. The weaker we feel, the harder we lean. And the harder we lean, the stronger we grow spiritually, even while our bodies waste away. To live with your "thorn" uncomplainingly—that is, sweet, patient, and free in heart to love and help others, even though every day you feel weak—is true sanctification. It is true healing for the spirit. It is a supreme victory of grace.[1]

MEETING GOD IN THE MIDST OF YOUR STRUGGLES

by Jodi Snider

Years ago, I used to be one of *those* people—one of those crazy people who got up at five in the morning and ran to their heart's content, which for me was usually seven miles. I'm not gonna lie—the first mile was always rough and would leave me scolding myself for ditching my comfy bed beside my sweet, sleeping husband. But I was always determined to push through so I kept going, and as I did, something beautiful would consistently emerge. Once that first mile was behind me, my body would settle into a sort of cadence, which freed my mind to let go of the battle of the struggling workout. I loved that release, so I would run. And run. And run.

Now, this was back before everyone had earbuds in every pocket of every outfit they owned, but honestly, I wouldn't have wanted that loud distraction anyway. For during those beautiful cadences where my feet fell into a perfect rhythm, my heart fell into line also. It was my quiet time to pray for guidance, pour out my heart, hear his voice, surrender control to my Savior, and get centered on his will for my life, all before most people's alarms ever went off. The silence that surrounded those runs was sacred to my daily routine.

Sigh. I miss those runs.

These days look much different (and I'm no longer one of *those* people). Disease has taken over my body and has even stolen my ability to choose my physical activities. On a good day, I wouldn't be able to walk a mile, much less run one. Oh, how my heart misses those active days! Tears fall hard just thinking of the freedom and physical strength God blessed me with so many years ago. I would be lying if I said I didn't miss things about that time in my life.

Yet even though my God has allowed such suffering and such difficulty to enter my world, I wouldn't go back to my old life, before he so beautifully wrote sickness into my life's script. That might not register with you, but especially if you are walking a hard road today, hear these words, dear one: I am grateful and thankful for God's amending to my life (sickness, disease, and all), for it has opened up such sweet worship opportunities and cherished moments of intimacy that could have only been drawn out from my utter brokenness.

You see, my physical strength may have dissipated, yet it has been so graciously replaced with complete dependence on the strength from my God—my strong tower. My legs may no longer be able to settle into that running cadence of years past, yet my Father has shown me I still have a deep-rooted need to synchronize my heart. So, a new routine emerged—it is grace-filled and it is raw. There's usually a pinch of frustrated tears and a helping of sorrow. Yet it's topped off with heaping amounts of praise and ends with submission to his will. And do you know what? It's just as sacred and just as beautiful as it was all those years ago. (Plus, I don't have to immediately shower afterward from sweat pouring everywhere, so I'm kinda partial to my modern-day bed worship.)

On those runs, I would never have envisioned this would be my story, yet I'm so grateful for a God who loves to pick up the pieces of our broken plans in order to create something more beautiful than my eyes could have ever taken in. He knows me so intimately that although my suffering and pain are surely hard for him to allow, he knows what is needed to get my heart back into the cadence of his will. And yes, some days are hard. Some days are painful. Some days I just want to quit, and hole up in my room and cry for all I have lost. Yet, as with that hard first mile, I am reminded that if I keep placing one foot in front of another as I trudge along this rough terrain, he will tune my heart to his voice, and rhythm follows. He will guide me so I won't gash my foot against a stone (Ps. 91:12). And whenever disaster strikes, he will protect me under his secure wing (Ps. 57:1).

Although running was great for my body, my brokenness has been best for my soul. And I'm thankful for a God who wants only what's best for me—to cling to his side no matter what may fail.

A PERSONAL WALK WITH JESUS

Even though life continues to move at a dizzying pace, I make time for prayer walks. These are times when I am intentional about blocking out the distractions of my day-to-day life, focusing solely on a conversation with my daddy in heaven. I love this creative method of prayer, because observing the wonders of nature reminds me how big and awesome God is compared to my problems. He is clearly reflected in the world around us (Ps. 8:3–4, 19:1–6; Rom. 1:19–20), and he can move the most daunting of mountains (Matt. 17:20).

Often I pause during my walks, look for a place to sit, and ponder the sights around me. I don't always, but sometimes I take a journal and jot my thoughts about how the things I'm seeing remind me of my faith. I might pick up a leaf, a rock, or a flower along the way to stick in my journal for that day.

I encourage you to explore a prayer walk of your own. If your phone is a distraction, consider leaving it behind. When I suggest this to my children and they immediately balk at not being connected, I remind them their father and I actually had to talk into a phone that was connected to the wall by a cord when we were growing up—and not because the phone was charging. Emails and phone calls can wait. Imagine tucking your phone away as you focus on a really important conversation with a friend who needs your undivided attention.

CREATIVE CONTEMPLATION

There are a variety of ways to contemplate God's majesty and splendor as part of your prayer walk journey. Here are just a few ideas to help get you started:

- Write a phrase or verse on a rock with a Sharpie. Keep the rock to hold when you pray, stow it in your purse as a reminder of God's unchanging Word (Ps. 119:89), or give it to a friend as a way to pray over them.
- Pick up a leaf or flower from your walk. In your journal or your Bible, write about how the detail of this small piece of God's creation reminds you of how precious you are to him. God is a God of details, and you can trust him in all things (Prov. 3:5–6).
- You might use that same leaf or flower to create a rubbing in your journal. Place the leaf or flower beneath the page and gently color over it with a crayon or colored pencil. Add notes around or over it. Think about the different textures and shapes. How do the varying characteristics of the nature you observe reflect the creativity and imagination of God?
- Sit quietly in your favorite spot outside, close your eyes, and listen to the sounds around you. Psalm 148:1–6 talks about how nature brings praises before God. Listen, observe, and offer your praise alongside the nature surrounding you.
- As you walk, ask the Holy Spirit to draw your focus to a tangible sign that will give you an idea of how you should pray for someone or something. In an earlier chapter, I mentioned a friend who hears the Holy Spirit speak through a number, which she may see on a billboard, a license plate, or even the balance of her Starbucks card. The Holy Spirit speaks to another friend through the symbol of a heart, which she's even seen in the creative form of bird droppings. And who said God doesn't have a sense of humor?

Try one of these ideas as you incorporate a prayer walk into your quiet time with God. As an extra treat, check out Part Three of this book, where you will find another coloring sheet designed to encourage you take in the world around you, pausing to acknowledge the splendor and majesty of God's creation. Go crazy with your colored pencils and add your own notes about the wonders you experience within nature.

Loving and gracious Savior,

We come to you in all our brokenness, in all our weariness, and in all our trials. This life we live doesn't always look like our hearts had envisioned, and it can leave us feeling frustrated and alone. Lord, speak into our hearts as only <u>you</u> can. Speak your truth as we do our part to dig into your Word daily and help us consistently seek you above all healing, above all saving, and above all need.

Fill us with your guidance and strength as we maneuver these new scripts you have written into our life's stories. And Lord, help us eventually come to a place of praise, even amidst the brokenness and even amidst the tears. Thank you for holding us on those days as we cry and for loving us enough to capture every tear in the palm of your merciful hand. You are a good, good Father, and help us never forget your goodness. It is in that mighty and good Name we pray.

Amen

—PRAYER OFFERING BY JODI SNIDER

THE
LORD
everlasting
God
THE
Creator
of the
ends
of the
earth
ISAIAH 40:28

CHAPTER EIGHT

Creative Intercessory Prayer

It was the fall of 1990, and I was a freshman in high school. Christmas was quickly approaching, along with the annual holiday celebration my extended family held every year. My grandparents, my mom, and my aunt usually cooked for months ahead in preparation for that special holiday weekend. The dining room overflowed with tables and tables of food, both savory and sweet. Each person had a favorite treat, and my grandparents always ensured no one was disappointed when the final spread was laid out for all to enjoy. Some of my very best childhood memories were made during these annual family Christmas celebrations.

However, Christmas that year was different and more somber than any holiday we'd previously shared together. The three oldest grandsons and my dad were missing from our annual family holiday gathering. My oldest brother and two of my cousins were deployed to Iraq for Operation Desert Shield, while my father was serving on active duty at Fort Polk, Louisiana.

Christmas morning also brought a new experience for my immediate family. While my father was able to spend Christmas at home with us, it was the first time my oldest brother had been away from home on

Christmas Day. My mom still smiled and laughed, but there was a poignant sadness about her. We still opened presents, but that was the first year presents were left under the tree, because my oldest brother wasn't there to open his. Even with the Christmas Day phone call my brother made to our family, even hearing his voice, it wasn't the same. His absence was felt deeply.

Just a couple weeks into January of 1991, the ground war broke out in Iraq. Operation Desert Shield became Operation Desert Storm, and my brother was on the front lines. My dad was at Fort Polk when my mom received the news. Craig, my other brother, and I came home from school to see friends consoling my mom in our living room. Eventually, everyone left. My mom told Craig and me to get in the car. We were going to church to pray for Chris, my oldest brother. We were going to pray for Joey and Todd, my cousins, who were also deployed. We were going to pray for the safety of all the soldiers away from home.

That was still a time when the church doors were left open so anyone could come to pray anytime they needed. Our pretty little Episcopal church sat on the bayou, the glass walls of the sanctuary overlooking a normally picturesque view. It was dark when we arrived that evening, so there wasn't much to see beyond the blanket of night. The only car in the gravel parking lot was ours. I dutifully knelt next to my mom and older brother as we prayed for Chris, Joey, Todd, my dad, and all the men and women who were facing the dangers of that war. I listened to my mom weep as she prayed, keeping my head bowed and my eyes closed. When she said amen, Craig and I helped my mom up and began to make our way out of the sanctuary.

We were almost to the car when I felt this overwhelming need to go back into the church and pray. This was a new sensation. I was no stranger to talking with Jesus, but this was something different. My mom agreed and continued on her way to the car with my brother.

I walked back inside, down the aisle to the steps of the altar where I knelt to pray. Then, I broke. I bent with my face to the carpet and sobbed, praying for the safe return of my oldest brother and cousins. I honestly don't remember how long I stayed and prayed. It might have been five minutes; maybe it was thirty. I don't remember. What I remember is that was the first time I felt an undeniable stirring in my spirit to pray for someone else. I was storming the gates of heaven in prayer on behalf of my big brother, my cousins, and my dad. This was my introduction to intercessory prayer.

WHAT IS INTERCESSION? DO I NEED A BAT PHONE?

Simply put, intercession is praying to God on someone else's behalf. The apostle Paul says in his letter to Timothy that Christians are to intercede for one another (1 Tim. 2:1). My mom, my grandmother, my aunt, my great-aunt, and pretty much all the women in my family before me were seasoned prayer warriors and often prayed to God on behalf of others. These ladies were known for their strength of spirit and often stood in the gap for others in prayer. No pressure, right? We used to joke with my mom when we had a prayer request, asking her to pick up her "bat phone" to call God. She would laugh and remind us that we have the same direct line to heaven that she did. And she was right.

JESUS THE HIGH PRIEST INTERCEDES FOR US

The best example we have for intercessory prayer was modeled by Jesus himself when he was on earth. He prayed collectively and individually for the disciples (Luke 22:32; John 17:6–19). He prayed for those who persecuted him (Luke 23:34). He prayed for you and me (John 17:20–26). Jesus is our high priest and continues to intercede for us in heaven (Heb. 7:25). However, if we want a deeper understanding of priestly intercession, we can flip to the book of Exodus, where we find further explanation of what intercession meant through the Levitical priesthood. I know that's a mouthful, but let's unpack it a little further.

In Exodus, Moses has led the Israelites out of slavery in Egypt into the wilderness. It's during this time in the wilderness that God reveals himself to Moses at the top of Mount Sinai (Exod. 19:1–3). A little further into the passage, we find Moses venturing back into the mountain to commune with God for forty days and forty nights (Exod. 34:28). It was during this trip that God imparted the Ten Commandments to Moses, so it's safe to say God and Moses were doing important work on the mountain.

We know from Scripture that even though the Israelites were God's chosen people, they were prone to wander and make questionable choices. Case in point, while Moses was on his mountaintop retreat with God, the Israelites grew restless in the base camp at the bottom of the mountain. They convinced Moses's brother, Aaron, to fashion a fancy gold calf for them to worship and indulged in drunken revelry (Exod. 32:6), which it's probably safe to assume wasn't your typical church picnic. The Lord saw what was happening and told Moses to get himself back down the mountain, for the people of Israel had corrupted themselves (Exod. 32:7). Before he left, though, Moses interceded with God on behalf of his people.

Have you ever said to your child, "You are *this* close to time out," or maybe the one I heard more frequently growing up, "Child, you are cruisin' for a bruisin'"? Friends, God was *out* of patience with the Israelites. Yet he relented and changed his mind about punishing his chosen people when Moses went to bat for them. In this instance, God said, "OK, Moses. I won't wipe their faces from the earth" (Exod. 32:14).

The people of Israel still faced dire consequences for their actions when Moses made his way down the mountainside. He was *unhappy*, to say the least, and we know that approximately three thousand lives were lost that day (Exod. 32:25–28). Yet, even after that, Moses went back up the mountain to intercede on behalf of God's wayward people (Exod. 32:30–32), because the people did not have direct access to God.

It was not long after the calf incident that God directed Moses to build a special place called the tabernacle, a *tent* or *dwelling place* with the purpose of reestablishing fellowship with Israel and serving as an outward and visible sign of God's presence. God gave elaborate instructions to Moses as to how the people of Israel should construct God's tent among them (Exod. 25–31). The Bible tells us that God appeared as a pillar of cloud over the tabernacle by day and a pillar of fire by night in the sight of all Israel (Exod. 13:21–22). The people would not set out on their journey unless the cloud lifted. It was an unmistakably powerful visual statement indicating God's presence among them. The tabernacle moved about the wilderness with the people. The Lord occupied a tent with tent dwellers.

The Israelites' act of disobedience when they fashioned that golden calf demonstrated their need to follow and worship a God who was visually tangible. God's provision of a tabernacle met that need and not only allowed the people to sense his presence, but also to see their leader go in to meet with God in a concrete place.

Aaron, Moses's brother, was from the Tribe of Levi and founder of the Levitical priesthood. You may remember all the people of Israel were descended from the twelve sons of Jacob (Gen. 49; Deut. 33:6–25). Jacob's third son was Levi, and Aaron was a fourth-generation descendant of Levi (Exod. 6:14–27). God designated Aaron and his four sons as the first priests. Aaron served as the first high priest in the tabernacle (Exod. 28:1). All of Aaron's male descendants in the tribe of Levi were chosen by God to serve as priests after him—thus establishing the Levitical priesthood (Num. 18:1–7).

In the tabernacle, the priest's responsibility was to serve as a mediator between God and the people of Israel. They stood between a righteous God and sinful people, bringing them together at the place of the blood sacrifice. To impress upon them the seriousness of sin, God set up a system of animal sacrifice for the Israelites in the Old Testament and required that the person offering the sacrifice lay his hands upon the *clean* animal to symbolize that it stood for him and his sins (Lev. 17:11).

God gave the Israelites the tabernacle and the sacrificial system so they could be absolved of their sins. So who is *our* mediator with God, and how do we know our sins have been absolved?

Jesus paid the blood price for our sins, and when the veil was torn during his earthly sacrifice, we were given access to God through the Holy Lamb. In the New Testament, John 1:14 says, "The Word became flesh and made his dwelling among us" (NIV). This word *dwelling* is the same word for *tabernacle* in the Old Testament. In other words, God came in living flesh to *dwell* or *become the tabernacle* among his people. As he walked upon the earth and lived among the Jews, Jesus Christ himself fulfilled the picture of the Old Testament tabernacle. In that and many other ways, the tabernacle really was a prophetic projection of the Lord's plan of redemption.

Matthew 27:51 says that when Jesus was crucified, "At that moment the veil of the temple was torn in two from top to bottom. The earth shook, the rocks split" (NIV). The veil became split, friends, so that we could become the ones to carry the Good News as the body of Christ. You are the tabernacle. I am the tabernacle. Because God dwells within us.

Jesus himself now serves as our high priest. There is no longer a need for a Jewish high priest to stand before the Lord and make atonement for our sins. Jesus has provided for our atonement through his death on the cross. See again why it's called the Good News? So now Jesus intercedes for us, and we are told to intercede for one another. "I urge you, first of all, to pray for all people. Ask God to help them; intercede on their behalf, and give thanks for them" (1 Tim. 2:1).

OTHER BIBLICAL EXAMPLES OF INTERCESSION

Examples of intercessory prayer are woven throughout the Bible, but let's take a peek at a specific few.

ABRAHAM

The people's sin in the cities of Sodom and Gomorrah was so flagrant, the Lord decided to destroy them. When God revealed his plan of destruction, Abraham interceded on their behalf and asked God to spare the people. Ultimately, God did not agree with Abraham, and the cities were demolished. However, Abraham still acted as a mediator between the sinful population of people and the Lord. We know God always hears our prayers and earnest petitions, but he does not always say yes to our requests.

STEPHEN, THE FIRST MARTYR

We meet Stephen in the book of Acts. In the days of the early church, spreading the gospel was dangerous (and in many parts of the world, it is still a dangerous calling). Stephen was one of seven men chosen by the disciples to help distribute food and care for the Hellenistic widows (foreign-born Jews who spoke Greek) in Jerusalem (Acts 6:1–6). But he went above and beyond the tasks he was given.

Stephen began preaching the gospel and was incredibly passionate about it (Acts 6:8–10). He was arrested on the accusations of false witnesses (Acts 6:9–14), and when he testified, Scripture says his face glowed like an angel's (Acts 6:15). Ultimately, Stephen was stoned to death, but as he was being pummeled with the stones of his accusers, he interceded on their behalf to God (Acts 7:59–60). Acts 7:60 says, "He fell to his knees, shouting, 'Lord, don't charge them with this sin!' And with that, he died."

EPAPHRAS

Epaphras was a Colossian who served as Paul's representative at Colossae and founded the church there (Col. 1:7). Described by Paul as a *beloved fellow servant* and *faithful minister*, Epaphras not only demonstrated intercessory prayer, but he was also likely gifted with a special calling for interceding to God on behalf of others (Col. 4:12). We should all be people of prayer, though some of us are specially called to a ministry of prayer, as Epaphras evidently was. Scripture tells us he prayed with persistence, perseverance, and specific, earnest petitions (Col. 4:12–13).

I know prayer warriors who feel *burdened* to pray earnestly and specifically for others. They set aside numerous hours each day to pray, because God has given them an undeniable urging to do so. This is not my spiritual gift. I love prayer and do pray often for others, but prayer warriors gifted with a calling for intercessory prayer are usually quite disciplined in their approach and the practice of interceding for others. Remember John Wesley and his prayer room?

It's important to mention again that even if we are not called to intercessory prayer as a ministry, Paul still tells us, "Pray in the Spirit at all times and on every occasion. Stay alert and be persistent in your prayers for all believers everywhere" (Eph. 6:18). You may not be setting your alarm for four in the morning, but even if the opportunity you take is to pray for others in the drive-through line waiting for your Frosty at Wendy's or in your car during your commute to or from work, the point is *you are praying for others* (1 Tim. 2:1).

A NUDGING FROM THE HOLY SPIRIT

The nudge for intercession comes from the Holy Spirit. Remember that unshakable feeling I mentioned about needing to pray for my eldest brother when he was deployed? Think about how often a name comes to your mind, or maybe the image of someone's face. Maybe it's someone you don't even know personally.

I love the testimony of Pearl Goode. In 1949, she was a widowed nurse in her mid-sixties. She ventured to a tent meeting in California, where she heard a passionate speech by a young evangelist named Billy Graham. She would later say in an interview that after hearing Billy Graham, "That night God laid those boys on my heart as a burden."[1]

She joined a volunteer prayer team and faithfully prayed over Billy Graham, the tent meetings, and the people who needed to hear the message that Billy Graham shared. This prayer warrior was said to have covered some forty-eight thousand miles by bus so she could be present to pray at these traveling revivals. Even after she could no longer physically travel, she remained engaged and committed to praying over Billy Graham when she knew he was going to be preaching.

Will Graham, Billy Graham's grandson, once said, "We must never underestimate the power of the prayer that is lifted up by wonderful saints like Pearl all around the world. Prayer—talking to God—is of paramount importance in developing our relationship with our Savior and in building up and supporting others through the work of the Holy Spirit. The great significance of prayer is—I believe—why we see so many calls to prayer in the New Testament."[2]

When you pray over others, you are storming the gates of heaven on their behalf. Galatians 6:2 tell us, "Share each other's burdens, and in this way obey the law of Christ." When we think back on how God has crafted us for community, it makes sense that intercessory prayer is a critical way to show love for one another, as some of life's pressures are just simply too difficult to bear alone (2 Cor. 1:8–11).

INTERCESSION IS WARFARE

Friends, there is a spiritual war being waged all around us (Eph. 6:12). The enemy who fights against us neither sleeps nor slumbers, but thankfully, neither does our Savior. If you are a believer, you're on the enemy's hit list. It really sticks in the devil's craw when believers want to bring the influence of the kingdom of God to earth as it is in heaven. Imagine him stomping his foot, with steam coming out of his ears, and foaming at the mouth. *You* do that to him when you honor the kingdom and take up the sword of the Spirit to do God's work here on earth.

Among my circle of writer friends, we are a praying and encouraging community. We live in different states and cities, but our common thread is our love for one another and a calling to share God's love through our words. Lately, we've noticed how amazingly determined the enemy is to bring each and every one of us down, and I'm not talking through a simple case of writer's block. I'm talking job loss, divorce, the arrest of a loved one, chronic illness—the *bring-you-to-your-knees-because-you-can-no-longer-stand* kind of tough life experiences. Remember Chapter Seven? We call it *life* happening, but it would be foolish of believers to ignore the war raging all around us. No, I don't believe Satan is behind every string of unfortunate luck, but he isn't idly sitting on the couch watching Netflix, either. Believers keep him very busy.

Satan's attacks are clever and calculated, and if we're being honest, the enemy occasionally scores a hit through our armor—for some of us more often than others. His goal is *always* to distract, divide, and destroy. He tempts and taunts us to succumb to the ways of the world, choosing wealth by worldly standards over wealth by eternal measure, choosing pride and anger over forgiveness and compassion. We defend against Satan's attacks by steeping ourselves in the Word of God and praying over one another and encouraging our communities to stand strong in the Spirit instead of the flesh. "For you have been called to live in freedom, my brothers and sisters. But don't use your freedom to satisfy your sinful nature. Instead, use your freedom to serve one another in love" (Gal. 5:13).

Intercession is a key battle strategy in the war against Satan, and fervent prayer is required if we are to resist the enemy's schemes and stand firm in our faith (1 Pet. 5:9). Pray, friends. *Pray*. Pray for your neighbors, even the ones who annoy you. Pray for those who have authority over you. Pray for our country and our country's leaders. When God places a name on your heart or brings a face to mind, *pause* and *pray*. Your words and your prayers hold great power. *Use* them. Jesus has already overcome the world (John 16:33), but the spiritual battle still rages around us. Our sorrows and struggles are temporary. Victory over the enemy is not; it's eternal.

Sandy Says

"When I read a Scripture—whether while participating in a Bible study, reading *Jesus Calling*, or through a verse someone shares—that grabs my spirit, I write the Scripture down on my index cards. At some point, not sure how many years ago it was, I changed the name of index cards and began referring to them as arrows to my quiver. Each Scripture *arrow* goes into my quiver to be pulled out and either fired into the enemy's camp or fired into the heavens as a prayer of intercession for someone."

INTERCESSION THROUGH THE EYES OF A PRAYER WARRIOR

by Kathryn McDaniel

"You are never more like Jesus than when you pray for others."

—Max Lucado, *Before Amen*

What a lovely thought that one of the ways to be most Jesus-like is to do something anyone can do. Anyone can pray; therefore, anyone can intercede on behalf of others. And we can be confident that God hears our intercessory prayers because the Bible explains how Jesus, our high priest, intercedes for us (Rom. 8:34; Heb. 7:25).

As I've grown in my faith, I've realized the incredible honor and gravity of interceding on behalf of others before our Lord. The Bible tells us in 1 Timothy 2:1–4 that "petitions, prayers, intercessions and thanksgiving be made for all people. . . . This is good, and pleases God our Savior" (NIV). It is an act that I know will matter, no matter the outcome.

Kneeling in prayer for others has always been an area of my prayer life where I've found comfort. However, the past two years have proven more challenging in this area as I've watched more loved ones battle pain, illness, deep grief, and sorrow. It seems I've gone to him more and more with petitions on behalf of my loved ones, waiting and watching for God to reveal how he was working in their lives.

Praying for my bestie (who is also the author of this book) has been a clear and precious picture of seeing God work, especially in times of greatest sorrow, and how he can deepen even the closest friendships through prayer for one another.

Cat and I met right after I graduated from Texas A&M. She interviewed for the intern position in the department where I worked, and not only did we get to work together; we shared an office. Instant connection doesn't describe strongly enough the beginning of our friendship. We look back now and can clearly see how God brought us together. But it would take several years into our friendship before we found another precious connection. Our mothers.

Now, our mamas didn't meet until a few years after we became friends. But every time they were together, they enjoyed each other's company. More and more opportunities popped up for them to spend time around each other. Eventually, they grew to love each other deeply and were blessed with special time together visiting the Holy Land. I truly believe that through our mothers' examples to us, their deep faith in their Lord and Savior, and their overwhelming love for their children, they set the stage for our authentic friendship. They themselves had shown us how to love and pray for friends, how to be there for others in times of crisis and sorrow, and how to live life with community.

I never fully realized the depth of these connections and their power until Mama Sandy was diagnosed with cancer. I had prayed

Cat through many tough seasons. She's shared many of those with you already. But praying for her, while I was also incredibly heartbroken and fearful at the same time, was tough. Those nine months were full of hope and lots of praying for miracles. We could all see Mama Sandy being held up by those praying for her. God gave her incredible strength to handle what this broken world threw at her. Her faithfulness through her last day on this earth was beautiful and precious to witness.

But now my sister was broken. It's so difficult, isn't it? To be side by side with someone you love deeply, seeing and feeling much of that pain, wanting to help them carry this immense grief and burden. My prayers sounded very similar those first weeks. I knew God was listening, but still I prayed for things repeatedly for Cat—comfort, peace, time to grieve leaning completely on the Lord, and also being surrounded by the people who loved her and could bring her joy. I knew I was doing the single most important thing I could be doing for her. God knew everything she needed, but still he desires us to come to him with everything.

Was I praying for exactly what she needed? Was I praying as God desired me to? I often start intercessory prayers with "Lord, if it's your will . . ." I trust in his will. I knew I needed to trust now and let the Holy Spirit guide me. And God, being God, gave me the words. He listened even when I stumbled on my words, knowing where my heart was at that moment. He led my prayers to change and grow as needed for the situation.

Through it all, as my prayers for her continued, my compassion for Cat deepened. My own grief gave way to my concern and love for her. God gave me unlimited patience and grace. He held me up, so that I could continue to hold her up through prayer. As weeks became months, when there was still much sorrow, God was there. The Bible tells us he hears his children as we cry out to him in prayer (1 Pet. 3:12). I have no doubt he heard. Even in the difficult moments, he heard.

Because here's what I saw.

He showed me a friend who was able to smile and laugh with me, through the tears. He gave Cat bravery to not retreat. The strength to show up when she didn't want to or felt like she couldn't. She has invested in her community *even more* in the past two years than ever before. She has a light in her now that shines even brighter. God revealed himself to us in his time, blessing her in ways he knew she needed.

As difficult as it is to trust God on days when there are rough seas, he wants us to continue to come to him, faithfully and fervently in prayer. He desires to hear from us regularly and not just on behalf of ourselves, but on behalf of others. He likens prayers to sweet-smelling incense in Revelation 5:8. What a joy it must be for him to hear our prayers of intercession and to witness us using his gift to be more like Jesus.

CREATIVE CONTEMPLATION

One of the creative ways I love to engage in intercessory art is through drawing and physically writing on the page the names of those I'm covering in prayer. Sometimes, the designs are abstract and resemble doodles with colorful names reflected in no order or pattern. I've also drawn a tree with the names of those on my prayer list reflected on each leaf. Yet another example of past ideas is the sketch of an ocean with the sun setting on the horizon, the names of those who need prayer represented in the ripples of the water.

Friends, the ideas for intercessory prayer art are limited only by time and imagination. I've included a creative intercessory prayer prompt for you to try and to help those creative juices begin to flow. Before you begin, though, read this verse again: "I urge you, first of all, to pray for all people. Ask God to help them; intercede on their behalf, and give thanks for them" (1 Tim. 2:1).

Take a moment to ask the Holy Spirit to place on your heart the names of the people who need your prayers today. When you're ready, begin adding a name to each flower petal, pausing as you go to pray specifically for that person. You may not know specifically how to pray for a name that comes to mind, and that's OK. If a name comes to mind, and you're unsure how to pray, invoke Romans 8:26–27 on behalf of the person on your heart: "In the same way, the Spirit helps us in our weakness. We do not know what we ought to pray for, but the Spirit himself intercedes for us through wordless groans. And he who searches our hearts knows the mind of the Spirit, because the Spirit intercedes for God's people in accordance with the will of God" (Rom. 8:26–27 NIV).

The design included here is just an idea and an opportunity for you to dip your toe into the waters of intercessory prayer art. Don't be shy about trusting your own God-given creative instincts. There's no shame in wanting to utilize prompts and templates, but I encourage you to try your hand at crafting a design of your own. However, if you want or need additional inspiration, Pinterest is a great source to browse. *Praying in Color* also offers really great guidance for creative prayer, and I highly recommend their method for intercession.

Father in Heaven,

An invisible war is unfolding all around us. Keep us aware and vigilant, Lord. Help us be responsive when the Holy Spirit nudges each of us to pray—especially when we are urged to pray specifically for someone or something. Convict our spirits to pause and pray regularly so that our prayers reflect a sincere offering of the call to action in 1 Timothy 2:1. Thank you, God, for the gift of salvation. We come before you boldly, unafraid to intercede on behalf of people the Holy Spirit prompts us to cover with prayer. Draw us all nearer to you, Lord.

In Jesus's precious name I pray,

Amen

Write a name of someone you are praying for in each petal of the flower. As you color each one, pray for that person!

CHAPTER NINE

CREATIVE PRAYING ALOUD

Moms and daughters who have been in Bible study with me and anyone who has heard me speak knows I often talk about the power of our spoken words. This is a message I am immensely passionate about sharing, especially in a day and age when people seem overly concerned with offending in person and vastly OK with tearing one another down from the safety of their computer screens and devices.

I was born and raised in the South, friends. As I've mentioned in earlier chapters, football and hospitality ain't no joke 'round these parts. While I was raised in Louisiana, I have always loved the Texas Aggies. *Always*. God was so good, too, because it was by his good grace that we moved to Texas my sophomore year of high school. And guess who was able to attend and graduate from Texas A&M University just like she had always dreamed? That's right, people. *Me*.

Yes, I know. Many, many people have a strong reaction when it comes to the Texas Aggies and not always in a positive way, but author and fellow Aggie grad Melanie Shankle will back me up here. College Station, Texas, really is one of the greatest places on earth. It might actually be one of the places where heaven and earth meet. Oh, and Jolie and Amie Sikes, founders of Junk Gypsy? Also Texas A&M grads. Are you sensing a theme here? Texas Aggies = awesomeness.

It's because I love my Aggies so much that I played the "Aggie War Hymn" on my way to work every single day when I was pregnant with my oldest daughter. You may call that crazy, but I call it *commitment*. The joke was on me initially, because the only thing that kept her from crying in the car after she was born was a small music box my best friend's mom gave her that played . . . you guessed it, the "Aggie War Hymn."

Fast forward five years or so to when Ashley was in kindergarten. At that time, we were still playing our biggest football rival, the University of Texas Longhorns. It wasn't uncommon to see maroon and white (Texas Aggie colors) and burnt orange and white (Texas Longhorn colors) represented among the students' choice of apparel in class. My big girl was fairly shy when she was younger and rarely had anything negative to say about school. Every day brought some fun, new experience that she couldn't wait to crawl into the car and share with her dad and me.

Well, one day I was waiting in the carpool line to pick up my daughter from school. As I inched closer to the pickup spot, I could see her standing off to the side with her little chin tucked into her chest. As soon as she climbed into her seat and lifted her face, I could see she had been crying.

"What's wrong?" I asked.

Her little chin quivered and a tear slipped down her cheek as she told me a classmate had called her a bad name during recess that day. When I asked her to share the word she had been called, she cried harder and told me it was too awful of a word to say aloud. I wracked my brain trying to think of what awful curse word could have been circulating the kindergarten playground that day.

Then I heard her soft voice say, "I think I could it draw it for you, Mommy." Really stumped now, I fished a piece of paper and pen out of my purse and passed them to her in the back seat. I waited quietly while she worked. Eventually, she handed the paper back to me. I stared at it, wondering what in the world this drawing was supposed to represent.

"Is it a ghost?" I asked.

"No, Mommy," she replied.

I turned the paper this way and that, hoping the answer would come to me. Then it dawned on me.

"Is it a longhorn?" I asked.

"Yes!" she cried, tears falling anew. "Isn't that awful?"

Trying my best not to laugh, all I could say was, "Aw, Doodlebug. I'm so sorry. That would have hurt my feelings, too."

My family may still chuckle about this story, but the fact remains. Words are not simply sounds caused by air passing through our voice boxes. God literally spoke the world into being by the power of his words (Heb. 11:3). The book of Genesis begins with the creation story when God said, "'Let there be light,' and there was light" (Gen. 1:3). As God's image bearers, we have power over words, too.

WITH GREAT POWER COMES GREAT RESPONSIBILITY

The Bible has much to say about the Lord's words as well as the power of our own. No word we speak is without significance (1 Cor. 14:10), so much so that Jesus says, "I tell you this, you must give an account on judgment day for every idle word you speak. The words you say will either acquit you or condemn you" (Matt. 12:36–37). Even the little kindergartener who called my daughter a *Longhorn* at school that day will have to stand before the Lord and give an account of his or her words. *Yes*, I'm poking fun at my daughter's experience, but the weight of our words is no laughing matter.

Wasn't it Peter Parker's uncle who said, "With great power comes great responsibility"? Whether you are Spiderman or not, Uncle Ben was right. That old phrase, "Sticks and stones may break my bones, but words will never hurt me" is a complete lie! Words have the power to encourage and beautifully transform a soul, just as words also have the power to corrupt and destroy.

We need only look back through history for evidence that words have the power to change an entire nation. For example, King Manasseh, whom we meet in the books of 2 Kings and 2 Chronicles, was an evil and cruel king. He was son of King Hezekiah and succeeded his father as the fourteenth king of Judah (2 Kings 20:21). The Bible tells us:

> He reintroduced all the moral rot and spiritual corruption that had been scoured from the country . . . rebuilt the sex-and-religion shrines that his father Hezekiah had torn down . . . worshiped the cosmic powers, taking orders from the constellations . . . burned his own sons in a sacrificial rite . . . practiced witchcraft and fortunetelling . . . in God's view a career in evil. (2 Kings 21:1–16; 2 Chron. 33:1–20 MSG)

His son, Amon, followed in the footsteps of his father (2 Kings 21:20–22). These two men led their nation away from God into the firm grip of corruption. Although Manasseh later repented of his evil deeds to God, the damage of his destructive rule was done.

Then came King Josiah, son of Amon, who became king at the tender age of eight when his father was assassinated (2 Kings 22:1). He was nothing like his father or grandfather. Josiah was a good king, who led his people in great spiritual renewal through the abolishment of idolatry and the restoration of the temple and worship, ultimately leading the people back into a right relationship with God. We know from Scripture, "He did what was pleasing in the Lord's sight and followed the example of his ancestor David. He did not turn away from doing what was right" (2 Kings 22:2).

All three kings would have communicated their laws and orders through the written and spoken word which, as we can tell, had a powerful effect on this nation. Leaders have the power to lead their people down a righteous path just as those in positions of power have the ability to lead their people astray, which King Manasseh, King Amon, and King Josiah's reigns illustrate for us. However, if we continue to peruse history for more examples of how people in power have influenced others through spoken language, we could easily cite their well-known, lingering words. Many such individuals use their positions of power for positive influence, people such as Mother Teresa, Mahatma Gandhi, Martin Luther King Jr., and Abraham Lincoln. We could even cite positive influences through pop culture, such as Bill and Ted (from *Bill & Ted's Excellent Adventure*), who said, "Be excellent to each other."

However, we could also just as easily cite well-known examples of people who used words to negatively influence the world around them, such as Adolf Hitler, Henry VIII, and Nero. There are plenty of pop culture examples we could add to this side of the argument as well, including the ugly words thrown by candidates and voters alike before, during, and after each election.

Now think about the power of words within the context of your own community. How frequently are words of affirmation spoken and shared? How quickly does gossip spread? Even as I type this, my mind is overflowing with examples from my own life, from my family and friends' experiences of how words have been used to both afflict and affirm. How many of us remember words spoken to us as children, whether shared in kindness or spewed in anger, that have stayed in our spirits well into adulthood?

In addition to the gift of language, God has also gifted us with the ability to make our own choices. *We* choose which words leave our mouths, a double-edged sword for sure (Prov. 12:18). If we let him, the Helper guides us, shutting our mouths to keep verbal barbs from injuring others around us, and inspiring our words as we open our mouths to encourage one another or pray.

Sandy Says

"Sometimes God is faithful in that he abruptly and without warning stops my swaying sword (tongue) from swaying out of control. Sometimes God is faithful and turns my swaying sword into a branch of peace. Sometimes God is faithful by allowing me to sway my sword to show me just how hurtful and destructive it can be when I sway instead of pray!"

THE HOLY SPIRIT DWELLS WITHIN US

Jesus asks us to abide in him (John 15:4), which we do through his Word (John 15:7). We abide in Jesus by spending time in the Word of God, but also by spending time in prayer. As Christians, the Holy Spirit dwells within us. The enemy does *not*. He does not *know* our thoughts or what is in our hearts, but he can *influence* our thoughts. Think back to how the Holy Spirit convicts, but the enemy condemns. The enemy influences our thoughts by spiritual whispers in the *ears* of our minds. That is why Paul tells us in Ephesians 6:11, "Put on the full armor of God so that you can take your stand against the devil's schemes" (NIV). We must use our spoken words to rebuke the enemy using the Word of God in Jesus's name.

Why does the Word of God hold so much power? I'm so glad you asked.

THE WORD BECAME FLESH

The apostle John tells us, "In the beginning was the Word, and the Word was with God, and the Word was God" (John 1:1 NIV). Look a little further into the first chapter of John at verse 14: "So the Word became human and made his home among us. He was full of unfailing love and faithfulness. And we have seen his glory, the glory of the Father's one and only Son" (John 1:14).

I love this. John was so clever in his writing. The Greek translation for *word* in this passage is *logos*, which was commonly used in both Greek and Jewish biblical cultures. Greek philosophers used the word *logos* to describe God at the beginning of creation, a force that created the cosmos out of nothingness and gave it order, form, and meaning. By introducing Jesus as the *Word*, John draws upon a familiar term and concept that both Gentiles and Jews of his day would have been familiar with. Just like Jesus used parables to teach, John finds familiar ground so the Good News is instantly relatable and understood by the people who need to receive the message of salvation.

John introduces Jesus as the *logos*, personalizing the Old Testament God, creator of the universe. John describes Jesus Christ as the *Word* (see also Rev. 19:13), and he further explains that Jesus, the *Word*, became a man to bear witness to the truth (John 18:37). Jesus is the Truth (John 14:6), the personification of the written and spoken Word. In the Old Testament, God revealed his Word through prophets like Elijah, Isaiah, and Haggai. In the New Testament, the Word of God is revealed in a Person, and that Person is Jesus Christ, the Son of God. And Jesus performed miracles, yes, but the primary way he spread his teachings was through the use of his spoken words.

Yet the Word is not only reflected in the Person of Jesus Christ; it is also reflected in the written Word of God—the Bible. We know all of Scripture is God-breathed (2 Tim. 3:16–17). Even though Jesus's life and teachings are only represented in part of the Bible, it is *all* divinely inspired. This is why the spoken Word of God is so incredibly powerful. When you speak or pray aloud the Word, you are tapping into the power of *Logos*, which is the power of Jesus Christ, the power of God.

THE POWER OF A WORD

by Lauren Gaskill

POWER IN HIS NAME

Hot tears flow like silent prayers from my swollen eyes. Each one whispers, *Jesus, Jesus, Jesus.* The pain, it's growing louder now—so loud I can barely hear my husband say, "It's going to be OK."

Is it going to be OK? Fear whispers from the back of my mind. *This could be it. This could be the start of everything breaking apart. You knew this day would eventually come. You can only outrun time for so long.*

Twitch. Pop. Spasm. There are little fires burning in my muscles, joints, and bones, torching an already fragile ecosystem. I open my eyes to stare at the blank ceiling, and this time I say it out loud, "Jesus. Jesus. Oh, help me, Jesus."

It's all I can muster, but for right now it's enough. Because, friend, there is power in the name of Jesus, and don't you ever forget it. For everyone who calls on the name of the Lord will be saved (Rom. 10:13). And at the mention of his name, demons are cast out and signs and wonders are performed (Mark 16:17; Acts 4:30). There is power when we call, mention, and pray the name of Jesus out loud amid our struggles.

Sometimes when we're hurting, the name of Jesus is the only thing our lips can utter. And that's OK, because his name is more than enough.

POWER IN HIS WORD

Later that night, my husband and I climb into bed, and I pull out my bedside Bible, desperate for a fresh dose of hope and truth. While dinner and dessert had offered welcome (and delicious) distractions for a few hours, the fear is returning as I settle under the covers.

Lord, give me a Word that will banish this fear once again, I pray.

I've read Psalm 91 more times than I can count, but I don't question when the Spirit leads me there once again. Tonight, however, it's not enough for me to simply read this passage of Scripture. You see, I don't just want the atmosphere of my mind to change. I want the atmosphere of the *whole room and house* to change. I want hope and faith to arise in such a way that the fear will flee with each spoken word.

"So, faith comes from hearing, and hearing through the word of Christ" (Rom. 10:17 ESV).

Even when believing is hard, God can deeply strengthen our faith and drive out fear when we dive into his Word.

POWER IN OUR PRAISE

It's morning now. The little fires have calmed down to embers, but still the aches and pains persist. I rub my eyes and debate whether or not I should even get out of bed. Mondays have never been my cup of tea, and this one is already shaping up to be a doozy. I hit snooze on my alarm and close my eyes as I roll onto my good shoulder to drift back to sleep.

Get up.

"Lord, can't you see I'm trying to sleep? You say to take care of the body you've given me, and that's exactly what I'm trying to do here," I say, clearly annoyed by the early morning disturbance.

This is the day that I have made. Rejoice, and be glad, Lauren (Ps. 118:24).

I open my eyes once more to see sunshine peeking through our blackout curtains. Still, all I want to do is stay in bed so I can drift into a state of being blissfully unaware of my pain. I try to cover my head with a pillow to block out the light, but when I do, one word flashes in my mind. *Rejoice. Rejoice. Rejoice.*

"OK, OK, OK, Lord!"

I grab my phone and tiptoe across the room while pulling up one of my sweet mama's favorite hymns, "Victory in Jesus." Ten years ago, if you'd asked me to sing a song of praise to my Savior, I would have jumped at the opportunity. Growing up, I sang on a daily basis and was a regular member of our church band. You know those crazy people you see sitting in the car next to you at a red light, singing their lungs out to the radio? Yeah, that was me. But that was before hypermobile Ehlers-Danlos destroyed my jaw and landed me with a stage-four degenerative joint disease diagnosis back in 2015. Now singing is a point of pain for me and a reminder that, while I don't understand all of the reasons, God has chosen not to heal me . . . yet.

But every now and then, as he has on this particular morning, he stirs in my heart to sing anyway. So, despite the fact I feel like my whole body has been hit by a car, I clear my throat and begin to sing that beloved hymn. While the pain hasn't yet left my muscles, joints, and bones, the blood of Jesus brings my heart to wholeness as I remember the ultimate victory I have in him.

A POWERFUL COMBINATION

Friends, we've established by now that prayer is powerful. Spoken words are powerful. The Word of God is powerful. Think about what happens when we combine all three.

In the Bible, the tongue is often compared to a sword (Ps. 57:4, 64:3; Prov. 12:18). Swords were the primary weapon in the ancient world, and the tongue is our primary weapon in the spiritual war raging around us. "For the word of God is alive and powerful. It is sharper than the sharpest two-edged sword, cutting between soul and spirit, between joint and marrow. It exposes our innermost thoughts and desires" (Heb. 4:12).

Praying aloud allows you to wield the sword of the Spirit (Eph. 6:17). When we leave the Word of God unspoken, we leave our sword in its sheath. Only God knows your innermost heart and desires. When you are praying to God, you needn't speak aloud for him to hear you. And there is nothing wrong with praying silently. (Jesus did, too.) However, praying aloud, especially when utilizing the Word, enables the unseen spiritual forces around you to hear your prayer, and they tremble at Jesus's name (James 2:19).

Not everyone is comfortable praying aloud. That's an understatement, right? I have friends who break into a full-body sweat at just the thought of having to speak in front of a group of people. If you are uncomfortable saying prayers out loud, praying the Scriptures aloud is a great place to start.

You also don't need to be in a group to practice. Remember my good friend Priscilla Shirer? In a scene from *War Room*, she rebukes the enemy in her home and kicks him square in the rumpus. Then she opens her back door, steps onto the patio, and says, "And another thing . . ." She knows he is gone from her house, because she has spoken aloud in Jesus's name and commanded him to go. So in order to keep the enemy on the run, she follows him out the door. This particular scene from the movie is a powerful visual demonstration of how to use the Word of God to push back while saying, "Not today, Satan."

POSITIVE INFLUENCE

Using our words through prayer can also influence others around us. When Paul and Silas were jailed in the book of Acts, we learn the prisoners and jailors heard them praying and singing hymns (Acts 16:25). God can use these opportunities to sow seeds of faith to non-believers. Christians are those whose hearts have been changed by the power of God, a change reflected in our words. Praying aloud allows others to hear your worship and set an example of one way someone else may talk with God.

We know there are other ways God communicates his power and might, right? There's the parting of the Red Sea, Daniel's escape from the lions' den, and the Houston Astros winning the World Series, to name a few. However, prayer and more specifically praying out loud, can also demonstrate the awesomeness of God in an undeniably impactful way. As E. M. Bounds said, "God shapes the world by prayer."[1]

POWER IN NUMBERS

Many of our spiritual battles have to do with relationships. That is why it is critical that every believer becomes a functioning part of a local church body or group of believers where others also see the world from a spiritual point of view. We need meaningful relationships that reinforce our spiritual life. Remember Bobbie Schae talking about the yearning for a Christian partner in faith? We're wired this way intentionally.

My husband and I are really blessed to have a close-knit tribe, four families who are doing a lot of daily life together. This isn't our church community, either, as we all belong to different denominations and houses of faith. These friends are like-minded believers who encourage and hold one another accountable as we strive to live a life of faith in a world that relentlessly tempts us to do otherwise. My girls refer to my mom friends in this group as their other mamas, and I've heard them say the other kids are more like brothers than friends. Not a day goes by that I don't feel so incredibly grateful for this group of people. However, of all the wonderful attributes reflected in our friends-we've-chosen-as-family community, the one I remain most thankful for is the fact that we consistently pray for and with one another. There is nothing more impactful, no greater gift we can offer one another than the act of prayer.

"Take this most seriously: A yes on earth is yes in heaven; a no on earth is no in heaven. What you say to one another is eternal. I mean this. When two of you get together on anything at all on earth and make a prayer of it, my Father in heaven goes into action. And when two or three of you are together because of me, you can be sure that I'll be there" (Matt. 18:18–20 MSG). The act of praying together brings us into God's presence in a fuller dimension than when we pray alone. There's a reason Jesus compared the kingdom of heaven to a banquet, rather than a tiny table for two. As a people crafted for community, life experiences are meant to be shared. This includes prayer.

Technology also provides a means for us to invite others beyond our physical proximity into the prayer circle. I mentioned my writing friends earlier, along with the fact that we live in different cities and states. In addition to regular phone calls, we keep in contact through two apps called Voxer and Marco Polo. We have used these methods of communication to pray over one another. The great thing about these two apps is the ability to set up groups. This means while one person may initiate the prayer, others often join and add their own words for the individual or group we are covering in prayer.

One friend in particular is really struggling; her life recently shattered into pieces in a matter of days. There are times when we feel at a complete loss as to how to pray for her. When this happens, we begin recording a message in the group chat, sometimes in silence; the only sight and sounds are our tears for our friend, reminding her that even when we don't have the words, the Holy Spirit is interceding on her behalf (Rom. 8:26–27). It takes intercessory prayer to another level when we are able to invite others through our phones, our computers, or our social media pages to join us as we storm the gates of heaven with intercessory prayers.

CREATIVE CONTEMPLATION

Today, think about the power of your words. Included here is a sample prayer as a resource to help you practice praying out loud. Another can be found in Part Three at the end of this book.

There are also quite a few praying aloud resources on the market. A few of my favorite are: *Adventures in Prayer* by Catherine Marshall, *Praying God's Word* by Beth Moore, *Praying in the Presence of Our Lord with Mother Teresa* by Susan Conroy, and *The Complete Works of E. M. Bounds on Prayer* by E. M. Bounds.

Like liturgical prayer, prewritten prayers can be a beautiful offering. Perhaps try your hand at writing your own prayer and then pray it aloud. I volunteered for years with the Vacation Bible School (VBS) at my church in a role called a "Sing and Play" leader. Those crazy volunteers who stand in front of all the kids at the beginning and ending of each VBS day, leading everyone in singing, dancing, and skits? Yeah, that was me.

The dancer in me loved it, but the anxious prayer-er within me did *not*. I got into the habit of writing my prayers before I'd have to stand and pray over the VBS kids and crews. Over time, I became more comfortable, and I also realized I wasn't the only one writing my prayers ahead of time. There's no shame in the prayer circle. Your words are powerful, friends. Use them wisely and remember your words could make the difference between adding another brick in someone's foundation of faith or leaving a scar deeply embedded on another's heart. Be a light. *Always* be a light.

Mother Teresa said, "We must live life beautifully; we have Jesus with us and He loves us. If we could only remember that God loves us, and we have an opportunity to love others as He loves us, not in the big things, but in the small things with great love, then (our country) becomes a nest of love . . . a burning light of peace in the world."[2]

Father God,

Please let our words be a source of encouragement to others who need them, to those who are lost, to those who feel oppressed by the darkness. Let them know they always have a friend in you, Lord. Help each of us to be the kind of friend who reaches first for compassion and understanding, using the powerful gift of language you've given to reaffirm our own identities as well as others in you. We are not rooted in the ways of the world. Thank you for the knowledge and authority of the name of Jesus, which you've given us to defend against the enemy's snare.

Help us give selflessly to our communities and beyond, especially to those who do not yet know of your unfailing love and grace. Use each and every one of us, Lord, as a mouthpiece to help others come to know you and to proclaim the glory of your name.

In Jesus's precious name,

Amen

A PRAYER TO READ ALOUD

Father God,

When they were jailed, Paul and Silas set an example to the other prisoners of what it means to sing your praises and worship you. Help me live my faith as boldly as they did so that I may encourage others who are prisoners to the ways of this world, that through singing your praises and worshipping you, they may come to know the fullness of your grace.

Forgive me where I fail you, Lord.

Please send your Holy Spirit to guide and teach me. Please also give me an insatiable hunger for your Word, becoming a more diligent disciple ready to serve when you call my name.

Thank you, God, for the love you give.

In Jesus's name I pray, Amen.

CHAPTER TEN

A Non-Crafty Girl's Guide to Creative Prayer

One of the ways I cope with stress is by coloring or crafting. My friends who aren't so crafty usually identify my level of stress by the type of crafting that occurs. For example, I frequently sit on my patio and color. This is immensely relaxing for me, and I love to shade and draw as I listen to the sounds of nature around me. It's not at all uncommon to find me tucked away with my Bible or a coloring book and my colored pencils. My non-crafty friends refer to this as DEFCON 3, the lowest state of stress for Cat. At this level, I still respond to texts and phone calls.

At DEFCON 2, the art supplies become a little more complex. This might include painting, hot glue, and glitter. I venture away from the traditional paper canvas as well. Travis Bird becomes a little nervous at this level, because I begin exploring Pinterest projects and paint chips. This means it likely won't be long before he's asked to craft as well. My non-crafty friends say at DEFCON 2, while I am still responding to texts and phone calls, I'm not likely to respond as quickly or frequently. Stress at this level is moderate, but Cat is still coping.

Lastly, there is DEFCON 1, the highest level of stress. When Cat hits this level, the Cricut machine is fully operational. The vision board is on display, and Cat leaves her phone plugged in by her bed most of the day. At DEFCON 1, Cat is deeply embedded in her introverted "hidey hole." Prayer is needed as well as chocolate. Texts and phone calls are directed to Travis Bird.

The first time I heard this, I laughed long and loud. Then I realized. *Uh-oh*. They weren't kidding, and as I thought more about it, I realized how accurate these descriptions are. Remember how awesome I said my tribe is? Look how well they know me, and they love me in spite of my quirks and DEFCON stress levels. The truth is that we all have our quirks and hang-ups, but we still crave to be loved in spite of our imperfections. It's such a gift when we find a community who loves well like this.

None of us is perfect. Jesus is the only perfect human ever to have walked the face of the earth. However, while none of us is perfect, we are all created by God with purpose. The original Master Artist sculpted each and every one of us, delicately instilling unique personalities, talents, and spiritual gifts. We are all God's workmanship, created in Jesus Christ for good works (Eph. 2:10).

CREATIVITY COMES IN MANY FORMS

We discussed this in Chapter Six, but it bears repeating. Creativity is expressed in vastly different ways, which might look like singing, dancing, writing, nature, fashion, and the list goes on. We briefly explored how Solomon creatively applied wisdom, how Tabitha creatively served her community with her seamstress skills, how David expressed creatively through song and dance, and how Jesus utilized creative teaching methods to share the gospel.

Let's take a peek at few modern examples of how creativity may be expressed beyond arts and crafts. Remember, creativity is multifaceted. Just because you may not be able to draw a straight line or create perfect origami, it doesn't mean you are uncreative.

THE CONTESTANT CHEFS ON CHOPPED—OR CHEFS, IN GENERAL

Chopped is a television show in which contestants compete on their ability to create dishes with the unusual combinations of ingredients they've been provided (such as squid ink, balut eggs, or stinky tofu). There are three timed rounds, and contestants must come up with a recipe and successfully execute it within the timeframe allowed. And these creatively crafted cuisines are supposed to taste yummy using the strange ingredients, with which the contestants may or may not be familiar—although usually the latter is true.

I'm going to confess. I *like* to cook, and I find this program incredibly stressful. (*Hang on, I'm going to turn on my Cricut.*) Somehow the dishes created are successful most of the time. These kitchen connoisseurs are undeniably innovative. To be fair, though, chefs in general are typically creative with the dishes they create and the manner in which they present them. It takes a creative person to artfully blend ingredients into a tasty dish that looks equally appetizing on the plate. Chefs demonstrate creativity.

JAMES DYSON

James Dyson is a true modern-day inventor. Every time you use a Dyson Airblade hands-free dryer in a public restroom, think of (and thank) James Dyson. He has also created a bladeless fan, a number of crazy cool vacuum cleaners, and several other innovations, such as the ballbarrow.[1] I'm not exactly sure what the market is for a ballbarrow, but James Dyson is undeniably utilizing ingenuity. He is one creative dude.

WALT DISNEY

OK, yes. Technically, Walt Disney was a cartoon artist, but his creativity went so far beyond sketches on a page. Did you know that before finding success, Walt Disney was a high school dropout who was fired from his first job working at a newspaper because he lacked imagination and his boss said his ideas had no merit?[2] Walt Disney faced personal and professional struggles for several years before utilizing his God-gifted creativity to develop what is now an entertainment empire.

The first time my family visited Disney World, I'm not sure who was more mesmerized, Travis Bird and me or our kids. What an incredibly creative vision Walt Disney had to create such a magical place!

JEFF BEZOS

Friends, Jeff Bezos is the founder and CEO of Amazon, an online store that literally carries everything you could possibly want—from textbooks to unicorn glitter. It seems like Amazon has it all. No matter how you may feel about it, it's tough to deny that Amazon has revolutionized the online marketplace. Thanks to Jeff Bezos's creative business mind, I can "click and add to cart" anytime I want—something Travis Bird probably wishes I didn't do so often.

A BEAUTIFUL OFFERING

You are the daughter of a king, who is the creator of all the heavens and the earth. His imagination is painted beautifully in every sunset, every landscape, every smile, every laugh—his fingerprints are everywhere. It's so tough not to measure our standards by what the world says should be pleasing and perfect. As Christians, though, we know the way of the world isn't the way of Jesus (1 John 2:15). We must rely on God's truth and the fact that he loves us so much that he sent his one and only Son to die so that we might have eternal life with him (John 3:16).

My children have created many homemade gifts for me over the years. I treasure them more than anything that could have been purchased, because these gifts were made by my babies' hands as a love offering to me. That is what *prayer* is to God. It is our love offering to God, and it is *precious* to him. Sure, I appreciate the beautiful artistry of professionals, but the gifts my girls have made for me reflect who they are individually. Their fingerprints (sometimes literally) can easily be seen in every finished design. What may look amateur to the trained eye looks perfectly polished to me. I believe this is what God sees when we explore the creative aspects of prayer and offer them to him. He delights in our heartfelt efforts to please him and to know him better.

Even if the creative characteristics you share with our creator aren't reflected in the perfectly crafted Bible journaling entry or a beautifully worded prayer, remember your sincere, heartfelt offering is pleasing and perfect to him, your Father who loves you more than you could ever fathom.

Sandy Says

"Dearest Ones, remain wise in the Lord! Keep his Word precious to you. Hold fast to its truth. One day we will all be together and oh, what a glorious day that will be!"

YOU ARE A VALUED MASTERPIECE

by Tracy Steel

I am an art-lover. I've admired the *Mona Lisa* in the Louvre and wandered through Claude Monet's gardens in Giverny, France, drinking in the beauty of the flowers and lily pads he so accurately captured in varying shades of green and purple. And I have studied the details of the faces depicted in portraits by Rembrandt on the walls of the National Gallery of Art in London. Despite the differences in styles, the artwork of these well-known artists is appreciated and esteemed worldwide.

So when Cat first told me about this book and shared its title with me, I was stoked, thinking she was going to talk about these artistic heroes and their secret prayer lives. Instead, Cat mentioned something about my own art and incorporating it into my prayers, which made me a little anxious. Sure, Monet probably would have been a fan of Mod Podge. However, any mention of podge or paintbrushes makes me nervous. Cat can attest to this: yours truly is *not* a crafty girl.

I like admiring art, but creating it? I cannot hang out with a Cricut or crayons, for they stress me out. Elmer and his glue bottles laugh at me. And do not let me attempt to draw a portrait of you. It will not resemble you at all unless we view it in a darkened room. Even the hallowed Bob Ross would not think my "trees" resemble anything "happy." One of my crafting fails was even highlighted on a Pinterest disaster blog. Yay, me! Bob would *not* be impressed.

As Cat and I laughed about this and about my history of Pinterest crafting fails, we realized I may not be the only non-crafty gal reading this book. Be encouraged if this is you, too, because all of us are made in the image of our creative creator, God.

In contrast to the famous artists I mentioned, our creative efforts may be lacking any kind of luster or worldwide applause, but they are well-loved and well-known by God. Since we are made in his image, we are creating something with our lives regardless of whether we operate a Cricut with great zeal or color inside of the lines.

We have the Holy Spirit within us, equipping us to do every good work God has given us, whether our style is graceful like Monet or more abstract like Kandinsky (John 14:26; Eph. 2:10). So do not compare or feel that your prayers do not measure up to those of the artists who apply glitter and Mod Podge like a boss. Whatever God is calling you to create in the corporate world with spreadsheets or in the classroom with hugs, graham crackers, and lesson plans is its own type of masterpiece in the eyes of your heavenly Father and worthy of its own amen. And so, God wants to be involved in your creative efforts, whether it be with words, food, music, or fabric.

Prayer invites God in and is something we all can do. So "pin" this deep within your heart: *you are crafted perfectly to pray*. Crafty and non-crafty girls alike can talk to God about fails or successes. Prayer is about your relationship with God and not about your résumé before him. It is about growing in intimacy with your Father and not about you imitating the exact style of someone else's prayer life.

So just like a real artist draws the eyes of the viewer to a main focal point in a drawing or painting, allow prayer to draw the eyes of your heart and mind back to the main focal point of everything, which is God himself. As you near the end of this beautiful book, utilize and remember the fun and creative ideas Cat is providing to help you encounter your creative creator. Even I am going to try the connect-the-dot activity included at the end of this chapter and fill in the beautifully illustrated color pages, not with the hope of completing them perfectly, but in hopes of experiencing my perfect and loving Father as I work through them.

And if I mess them up, oh well. Nothing can separate you or me from the love of God (Rom. 8:38–39). Not spilt glitter or a bumbling or botched prayer. Or unhappy trees and a disappointed Bob. God simply wants the gaze of our heart to rest upon him, the intended focal point of our lives, and not upon the answer he may or may not provide. For knowing and enjoying God is what relating to him in prayer is all about. And there is no other safer or more powerful canvas upon which to create a real and satisfying relationship with God than prayer. So enjoy God and talk with him. Just like the infamous *Mona Lisa*, your prayers are famous in your Father's eyes and esteemed heavenwide.

Beautiful thought, isn't it? Better get busy, then, crafting some amens of your own, highly creative and valued masterpiece of God.

A QUICK LOOK BACK

While our creative exploration of prayer in this book is coming to an end, I pray your artistic expression of prayer with our Father is just beginning. Let's take a quick look back at how we've unpacked the practice and power of prayer throughout the pages of this book.

CREATED FOR COMMUNITY

In the first chapter, we unpacked the practice of prayer, what it is, and why we as a people crave connectivity. As the image bearers of a triune God, we are modeled for community. We are innately wired to be social, to share, and to bond with others in some meaningful way. One way we express our relational nature is through communication. *Prayer* is how we communicate with God, the creator of all things. We define prayer simply as an open, honest conversation with our heavenly Father, who longs for us to know him and rest in the assurance of his unfailing love and faithfulness.

WHY DO WE PRAY?

Healthy relationships consist of honest, regular communication, which involves both listening and speaking. Prayer enables us to have a relationship with God, which is further enriched through Scripture. We explored why we pray, examples of prayer as modeled by Jesus himself, and other biblical illustrations of men and women who prayed. George Müller, John Wesley, and Horatio G. Spafford provided more modern-day examples of what a "prayer warrior" looks like and why this practice is not only still applicable, but critical to our lives as Christians today.

We also learned that just like those who modeled prayer for us, each and every one of us is called to be a prayer warrior. There is a spiritual battle raging around us, and even though the war has already been won, the enemy is relentless in his pursuit of our families, of our livelihoods, and of us. Satan strives to distract, divide, and destroy. As God's image bearers, we have the power and authority in Jesus's name to rebuke Satan and the force of evil he commands.

The enemy would have us believe that our words do not matter and that prayer is pointless. We know nothing could be further from the truth. As the image bearers of a God who literally spoke our world into being, our words and our prayers hold great power, and that truth scares the pants off of Satan.

WHO IS THE HELPER?

In Chapter Three, we turned our focus to our Advocate (John 14:16–18), the Holy Spirit whose role in the life of every believer is quite multifaceted. Even though the Holy Spirit is referenced as an ethereal being, the truth is our Helper is an active, relational member of the Godhead. We have a personal relationship with the Holy Spirit just as we have a personal relationship with the other two persons of the Holy Trinity. And as image bearers of the Godhead, we share qualities with the Father, the Son, *and* the Holy Spirit.

From the moment we become a Christian, the Holy Spirit dwells within us—his purpose to lead us, to guide us, to help us do the things God wants us to do as we strive to walk in faith. The Holy Spirit approaches each of us in the way we will hear him best. There is no cookie-cutter way the Holy Spirit speaks, because we all hear and receive his voice differently. When he speaks, he convicts; he does not condemn. It takes practice and a willingness to hear the Holy Spirit. We must learn to know his voice.

DOES GOD HEAR AND ANSWER OUR PRAYERS?

Yes. He does. Always. Though he does not always say yes or answer our prayers in the timeframe we request. Jesus himself modeled for us how we should talk with God, and we see through Scripture that Jesus taught us to pray, "Not as I will, but as you will, God." Even in seasons when God seems silent, he is ever-present. Sometimes, children just need to be held. Our good, good Father in Heaven longs to hold us through stormy seasons of life. He hears every cry, every sob, and he holds every tear in the palm of his hand.

In this chapter, we introduced the Sunday House prayer, a way to bring your boldest, most bodacious prayers before God. When we pray and lay our dreams and heart's desires at God's feet, we trust and wait for him to show up in a way that only God can. Learning to lean deeply when God says no or not yet, we surrender to his perfect will, trusting him to answer our prayers in his time and his way.

A FRAMEWORK FOR PRAYER

A common hang-up with prayer is simply not knowing how or where to begin. Thankfully, the Bible gives us a clear framework for prayer—the Lord's Prayer. When asked by the disciples, "Lord, teach us to pray," Jesus did. Another obstacle to prayer is its place on our list of priorities. In a culture that encourages us to be connected more than ever before, and as we set our lives to the rhythm of rush, the most important relationship often falls to the bottom of the pile of *stuff*. Even the busiest Marthas are invited to lay their burdens down and rest at Jesus's feet.

In Chapter Five, we also walked through how to personalize the Lord's Prayer and explored a creative tool (G-R-A-C-E) to help organize our thoughts as we pray. As the One who created us, God already knows our hearts *intimately*. Sometimes it's tough, but we shouldn't get tripped up in making pretty words. Speak from your spirit, and the open, honest words from your heart will flow.

CREATIVE BIBLE JOURNALING

One of the most popular creative methods of contemplating Scripture today is Bible journaling. In our first creative method of the book, we explored how coloring and drawing might translate to prayer. Be encouraged to try your hand at taking colors to Scripture and inviting the Holy Spirit to work in your heart as you contemplate the words you've read.

Creativity is innately woven into God's character. The expression of creativity is versatile and provides ample opportunity to explore worship with God in a variety of ways. Traditional methods of prayer are beautiful, too, but Bible journaling offers us a creative way to share our hearts with God in a way that is just as deeply personal and impactful. Bible journaling is simple and affordable, and it begins with a longing to dig deeper into God's Word and develop a more personal friendship with Jesus.

CREATIVE NATURE WALK PRAYER

The Bible references the importance of caring for our bodies and the connection between physical and spiritual health. This creative prayer method is all about exploring an alternative to traditional prayer by combining prayer with physical activity like a walk. There are undeniable benefits to being still and sitting quietly at the feet of God. This creative method of prayer does not to diminish those quiet times at all, but rather offers another intentional way to spend time with God in prayer.

In our rhythm-of-rush lives, we can and should press pause with intention and shift our gaze to our heavenly Father with an attitude of worship. It takes spiritual discipline, which shouldn't invoke a negative response with regard to prayer and communion with God. We spend time in prayer because we *love* Jesus and want to know him better—not because we are afraid of punishment.

Many athletes train with a fierce determination, striving to cross the finish line or win the prize. Paul tells Christians that spiritual discipline is like the training of an athlete. The difference is we are sprinting toward an eternal prize—salvation and eternal life with our Lord and Savior. Pray regularly for God to give you a heart for discipleship, the hunger and passion needed for your spiritual training, and the strength and endurance to run your spiritual race.

CREATIVE INTERCESSORY PRAYER

Simply put, intercession is praying to God on someone else's behalf. Because we are a people designed for community, Paul's urging in 1 Timothy 2:1 makes perfect sense. Interceding for one another is just one of the ways we show love for our brothers and sisters, even the ones who step on that last nerve.

In Chapter Eight, we unpacked the foundation of intercessory prayer all the way back to the Levitical priesthood, when it was the high priest's job to intercede on behalf of the people to God. This job revolved around a sacrificial system given by God to Moses. A blood sacrifice was always required to absolve sin. Jesus paid the blood price for our sins on the cross, and when the veil was torn during his earthly sacrifice, we were given access to God through the Holy Lamb. Jesus is our high priest. There is no longer a need for a high priest to stand before the Lord and make atonement for our sins. Jesus has provided for our atonement through his crucifixion. This means the Old Testament tabernacle is no longer necessary, because God dwells within each of us. So we are free to approach God directly with our earnest petitions, but also for the needs and requests of others.

The nudge for intercession comes from the Holy Spirit and comes in the form of a name or face that suddenly comes to mind. Intercession is also a key battle strategy in the war against Satan, and fervent prayer is required if we are to resist the enemy's schemes and help one another stand firm in our faith.

The seriousness of the calling doesn't mean you can't enjoy a creative process along the way. Intercessory prayer art is vast and varied. Your prayers are powerful, friends. Remember, the point is not to create a perfectly illustrated piece of art. The point is you are praying and listening to the urging of the Holy Spirit when he prompts you to pray over someone or something else.

CREATIVE PRAYING ALOUD

Sticks and stones may break our bones, but words can never hurt us. We know nothing could be further from the truth. Words hold *immense* power. We know this because God literally spoke our world into being (Gen. 1:3). As God's image bearers, our words hold great power as well.

Together we explored the impact of praying aloud. God commands us to pray, but he also calls us to know him and to help make him known. Praying aloud allows others to hear our worship and set an example of one way someone else may talk with God. And for our friends who are still a little timid about praying out loud, be encouraged! There's no shame in reading a prewritten prayer, regardless of who authored the message.

The Bible compares the human tongue to a sword (Ps. 57:4, 64:3; Prov. 12:18). Swords were the primary weapon in the ancient world, and the tongue is our primary weapon in the spiritual war raging around us. Praying aloud allows you to wield the sword of the Spirit (Eph. 6:17).

Praying with your community magnifies the power of prayer and brings us into God's presence in a fuller dimension than when we pray alone. Remember, there's a reason Jesus compared the kingdom of heaven to a banquet, rather than a tiny dinner party. As a people crafted for community, life experiences are meant to be shared. This includes prayer. Use your words as a force for good, people!

Even as you close this book and venture on to another, I pray the message and the heart behind the words within these pages remain deeply imprinted on your heart. You are not a byproduct of the ways of this world. You are a daughter of the king, and you belong to Jesus. Rest in the assurance that you are intentionally sculpted—every hair, every follicle, every quirk, every aspect of you down to the tiniest detail is as such *on* purpose *with* purpose—by a creator who loves you more deeply and fully that you could ever imagine. How awesome is that? I pray this truth stays embedded in the core of your heart.

I pray you have an insatiable hunger to know Jesus better than any other relationship in your life and that this hunger to know and love him impacts every aspect of who you are, what you do, and where you go. Our faith is contagious in the best possible way, and I pray the tools within this book give you encouragement and inspiration to love others well and positively influence their walk of faith.

We all need community. Even though you may only walk with a person briefly in your journey of faith, you never know how the seed your words planted will take root, grow, and flourish. So spread kindness and your love of Jesus wherever you go—and maybe a little glitter, too.

CREATIVE CONTEMPLATION

Even the non-crafty girl can try her hand at creative prayer. Included here is a fun activity with a special message just for you. Rest in the assurance that you are uniquely crafted by a loving God with a special purpose. However your creative talents may manifest themselves and regardless of any past Pinterest fails, you *do* embody these traits as the image bearer of our creator.

Father God,

We come before you, and we lay all our failures at your feet. Our attempts at creating anything of beauty sometimes fall short, and we feel unseen or not enough sometimes. We give you our shame, our guilt, and our discouragement. Please fill us with your truth, your peace, and your joy, God. Draw us closer to you and help us find our worth and security in you and you alone.

Thank you for making us into your image and for all that you are helping us to do and be. And thank you for loving each and every one of us just as we are and for wanting to meet with us daily, whether our words are many or whether they are few. May the words of our mouths, the art of our hands, and the meditations of our hearts be pleasing to you, always (Ps. 19:14).

Amen

—PRAYER OFFERING BY TRACY STEEL

PART THREE

Creative Contemplation Extras

"PRAYER IS THE EXERCISE OF DRAWING ON THE GRACE OF GOD."

—OSWALD CHAMBERS, *MY UTMOST FOR HIS HIGHEST*

MORE CREATIVE PRAYER EXPERIENCES

1. Bible journaling traceables

2. Nature walk coloring page
(additional journal entry with Isaiah 40:28–31 and embellishments)

3. Luke 11:9 coloring page

4. Power of a Name coloring page

5. Hand-lettered read aloud prayer

6. Writing Scripture in your own hand for the non-crafty girl

Therefore
as you
received
Christ
Jesus
the Lord
so walk
in him
rooted
and built up
in
Christ
and
established
in the
faith
COLOSSIANS 2:7
Seek
His
will
in all you do
and
He
will
show you
which path
to take
PROVERBS 3:6 NLT

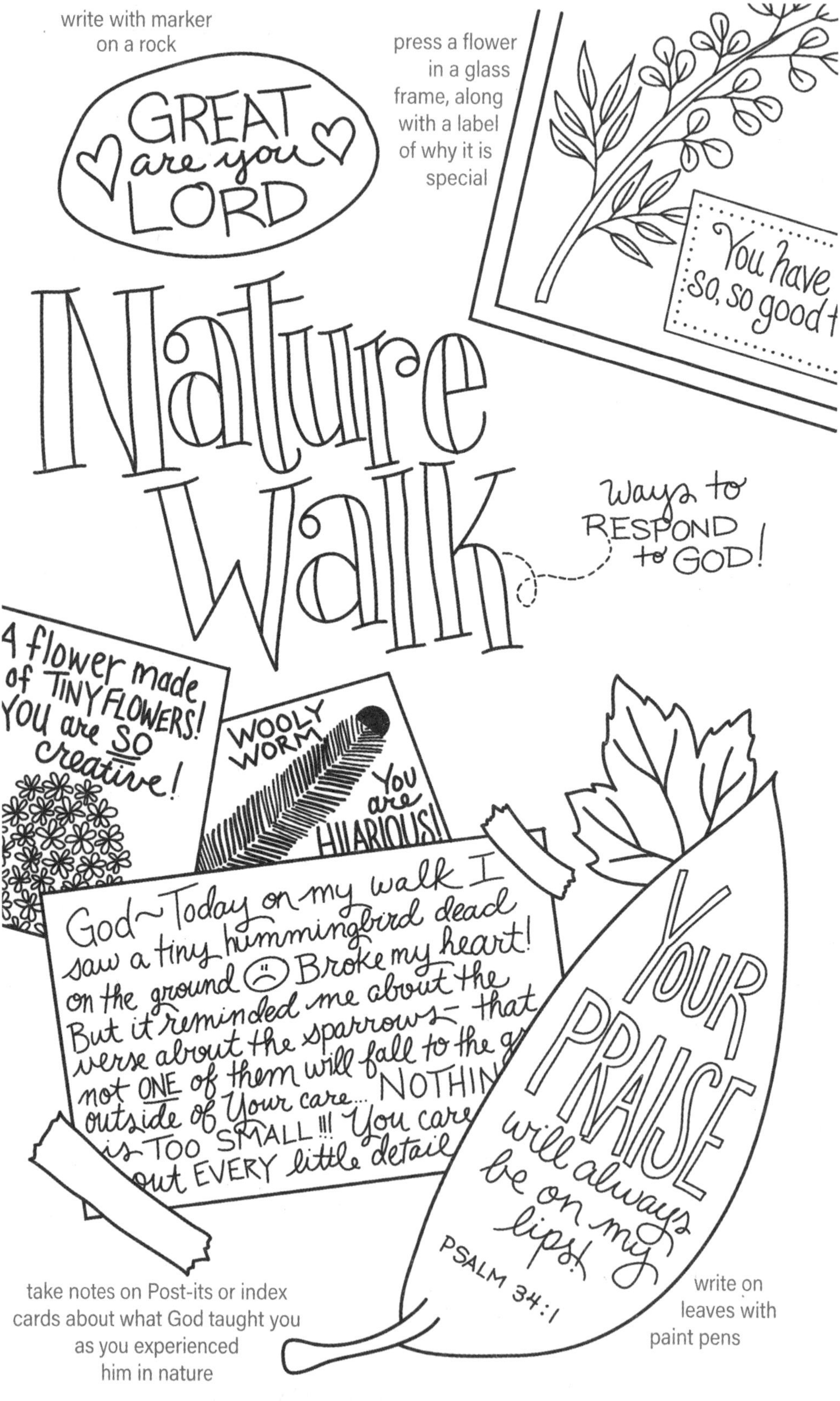
write with marker
on a rock
GREAT
are you
LORD
press a flower
in a glass
frame, along
with a label
of why it is
special
You have
so, so good
Nature
Walk
ways to
RESPOND
to GOD!
A flower made
of TINY FLOWERS!
YOU are SO
creative!
WOOLY
WORM
YOU
are
HILARIOUS!
God~Today on my walk I
saw a tiny hummingbird dead
on the ground Broke my heart!
But it reminded me about the
verse about the sparrows– that
not ONE of them will fall to the g
outside of Your care... NOTHIN
is TOO SMALL!!! You care
out EVERY little detail
YOUR
PRAISE
will always
be on my
lips!
PSALM 34:1
take notes on Post-its or index
cards about what God taught you
as you experienced
him in nature
write on
leaves with
paint pens

ASK
and it will be
GIVEN
TO YOU

SEEK
and you will
FIND

KNOCK
and it will be
OPENED
TO YOU

LUKE 11:9

THE NAME
OF THE
Lord
IS A
STRONG TOWER
PROVERBS 18:10
IMMANUEL
God with us
ABBA
Father
EL SHADDAI
God Almighty
God
EL ROI
who sees
YAHWEH
the Lord
YIREH
will provide
the
ELOHIM
One and Only God
Jesus Christ

A PRAYER TO READ ALOUD

My Father in Heaven,

You have shown that words hold great power.
You literally spoke our world into being, and as your image bearer,
I understand my words have great power, too.
Jesus also modeled for us how to use the spoken word
to rebuke the enemy, who trembles at his name.

Help me be a good steward of this powerful gift.
Let the words that leave my lips encourage and affirm.
Let the verbal barbs I utter be in defense against the enemy's schemes,
and help me wield the sword of the Spirit
like the prayer warrior you have designed me to be.

Forgive me when my words and actions fall short of honoring you.
Thank you for your faithfulness, your grace, and your love.
I love you, too, Father. I am yours.

In Jesus's name I pray,
Amen.

Kings in ancient Israel were commanded by God to write Scripture in their own handwriting. Use the space above to write out some verses that are particularly meaningful to you!

Deuteronomy 17:18–20 (ESV)

"And when he sits on the throne of his kingdom, he shall write for himself in a book a copy of this law, approved by the Levitical priests. And it shall be with him, and he shall read in it all the days of his life, that he may learn to fear the LORD his God by keeping all the words of this law and these statutes, and doing them, that his heart may not be lifted up above his brothers, and that he may not turn aside from the commandment, either to the right hand or to the left."

RESOURCES

BOOKS

Bassett, Erin. *The Art of Bible Journaling: More Than 60 Step-by-Step Techniques for Expressing Your Faith Creatively*. New York: Get Creative 6, 2017.

Chalkfulloflove. *Hand Lettering 101: An Introduction to the Art of Creative Lettering*. Bend, OR: Blue Star Press, 2016.

Fink, Joanne, and Regina Yoder. *Complete Guide to Bible Journaling: Creative Techniques to Express Your Faith*. East Petersburg, PA: Fox Chapel, 2017.

Inspire Bible. Carol Stream, IL: Tyndale, 2016.

NIV Beautiful Word Bible. Grand Rapids: Zondervan, 2016.

ONLINE INSPIRATION

"#biblejournaling." *Instagram*, https://www.instagram.com/explore/tags/biblejournaling.

Catherine Bird. "Bible Journaling." Pinterest collection, https://www.pinterest.com/catherinefbird/bible-journaling.

Melissa Fischer. https://fischtaledesigns.blogspot.com.

Rebekah R. Jones. https://rebekahrjones.com.

Sandy Allnock. http://sandyallnock.com.

Scrapbook.com. https://www.scrapbook.com.

Sybil Macbeth. https://prayingincolor.com..

A PRAYER-FULL PLAYLIST

by Tracy Steel

"Just pray about it."

Has this phrase ever inspired dread within you? It has within me! Sure, this is wonderful advice that we should heed, but let's be honest, sometimes the hardest thing about praying is actually sitting down, being still, and doing it.

I remember being told that praying "the right way" involved sitting still like a statue, bowing my head, and squeezing my eyes closed. So growing up, I didn't pray very much, because sitting still and bowing my head for a lengthy period of time was (and still is) an impossible feat for this busy and fidgety gal.

But something that does quiet my heart and hold my attention is music. I have always been a lover of it. So naturally, I turn to it whenever I struggle to pray. If you are unsure of how to pray right now, or if silence or sitting still scares or intimidates you, I encourage you to check out the songs on the following playlist. It includes some of Cat and my favorite praise and worship tunes. I use them as an aid for my quiet time. Cat uses them as she walks or doodles in her Bible. Worship music can be a beautiful offering of prayer.

Simply listen to the words, and if you know the lyrics, sing them or pray them in your heart back to God as an offering of your worship. Feel free to stand up and move or sway as you listen to the music and pray, with your arms lifted high and your eyes open wide. If some of the lyrics weigh heavily upon you, pause the song and talk to God a little longer about whatever the lyrics evoke within you. You may be prompted to confess something you are struggling with or praise God for a specific thing or person that the song brings to mind. And when the music is over, continue to pray as you feel led.

Music is potent, and while it can make us feel nostalgic, help us feel happy, or generate energy, we can also use it as a powerful springboard to help us become prayer-full as well. So enjoy and pray away!

Assad, Audrey. "It Is Well with My Soul." *Inheritance*, Fortunate Fall Records, 2016.

Battistelli, Francesca. "Holy Spirit." *If We're Honest*, Fervent Records, 2014.

Bethel Music. "It Is Well." *Without Words: Synesthesia,* Bethel Music, 2015.

Daigle, Lauren. "Come Alive (Dry Bones)." *How Can It Be*, Centricity Music, 2015.

Daigle, Lauren. "You Say." *Look Up Child*, Centricity Music, 2018.

Dixon, Colton. "More of You." *Anchor*, Sparrow, 2014.

Hillsong United. "From the Inside Out." *Mighty to Save: Powerful Songs of Transforming Worship,* Integrity Music, 2007.

Hillsong United. "Oceans." *Zion*, Hillsong, 2013.

Kerr, Hannah. "I Stand Here." *Overflow,* Black River Christian, 2017.

Maher, Matt. "Lord, I Need You." *All the People Said Amen*, Essential Records, 2013.

Nicole, Britt. "Walk on the Water." *The Lost Get Found*, Sparrow Records, 2009.

Passion. "Take My Life (Live)." Feat. Chris Tomlin, *Hymns Ancient and Modern*, EMI, 2004.

Plumb. "Beautifully Broken." *Beautifully Broken,* Centricity Music, 2018.

Shane & Shane. "Come Thou Fount." *The Worship Initiative, Vol. 1,* WellHouse Records, 2014.

Wickham, Phil. "At the Foot of the Cross (Acoustic)." *Children of God Acoustic Sessions*, Fair Trade/Columbia, 2016.

NOTES

CHAPTER TWO: WHY DO WE PRAY?

[1] Dr. Seuss Geisel, *Happy Birthday to You!* (New York, NY: Random House, 1987).

CHAPTER THREE: WHO IS THE HELPER?

[1] Sinclair B. Ferguson, *The Holy Spirit* (Downers Grove: InterVarsity Press, 1997), 12.

CHAPTER FIVE: A FRAMEWORK FOR PRAYER

[1] *Book of Common Prayer,* "Pater Noster," https://www.bcponline.org/General/paternoster.html.

[2] Annie Downs, *That Sounds Fun* podcast, episode 91: Steffany Gretzinger, minutes 20:04–20:08, http://www.anniefdowns.com/2018/07/27/that-sounds-fun-podcast-episode-91-steffany-gretzinger.

[3] Downs, *That Sounds Fun*, minutes 22:35–22:38.

CHAPTER SIX: CREATIVE BIBLE JOURNALING

[1] Ian Poulton, *For the Fainthearted* blog, "An A-Z of Hymnwriters: Joseph Scriven," https://forthefainthearted.com/2011/10/05/an-a-z-of-hymnwritersjoseph-scriven/.

[2] John Piper, *Desiring God* (Sisters, OR: Multnomah Publishers, Inc., 2003), 142.

CHAPTER SEVEN: CREATIVE NATURE WALK PRAYER

[1] J. I. Packer, *Hot Tub Religion* (Wheaton, IL: Tyndale House Publishers, 1987), 192–93.

CHAPTER EIGHT: CREATIVE INTERCESSORY PRAYER

[1] Will Graham, "Will Graham on Pearl Goode and the Power of Prayer," Billy Graham Evangelistic Association (website), May 5, 2016, https://billygraham.org/story/will-graham-on-pearl-goode-and-the-power-of-prayer.

[2] Graham, "Will Graham on Pearl Goode." The biblical calls to prayer he lists in the article include Luke 6:28; Rom. 12:12; Phil. 4:6; Col. 4:2; 1 Thess. 5:17; and 1 Tim. 2:8.

CHAPTER NINE: CREATIVE PRAYING ALOUD

[1] E. M. Bounds, *Purpose in Prayer* (New Kensington, PA: Whitaker House, 1997), 9.

[2] Phyllis Zagano, *Twentieth Century Apostles: Contemporary Spirituality in Action* (Collegeville, MN: Liturgical Press, 1999), 89–90.

CHAPTER TEN: A NON-CRAFTY GIRL'S GUIDE TO CREATIVE PRAYER

[1] CBSNews, "10 Awesome Inventions from James Dyson," https://www.cbsnews.com/pictures/10-awesome-inventions-from-james-dyson/8.

[2] Rachel Gillett, "How Walt Disney, Oprah Winfrey, and 19 Other Successful People Rebounded after Getting Fired," *Business Insider*, October 7, 2015, http://www.inc.com/business-insider/21-successful-people-who-rebounded-after-getting-fired.html.

About the Contributors

The following contributors agreed to come alongside me (and *you*) to share a piece of their hearts for this project, and I am deeply grateful. *The Art of Amen* would not be the same without each and every one of their voices. These are people I am so thankful to call friends and family, and you can read a little more about each of them here, as well as where to track them down online.

Ashley Bird is Catherine and Travis Bird's oldest daughter. She is a Jesus girl who loves her Australian Shepherd named Gatsby and all things dance. Currently, she is a junior in high school with her sights set on attending Texas A&M University. There she hopes to major in biomedical sciences before attending medical school.

Jen Ferguson is a wife, mama, author, and speaker who is passionate about helping couples thrive in their marriages. She and her husband, Craig, share their own hard story in their book *Pure Eyes, Clean Heart: A Couple's Journey to Freedom from Pornography*, and they are creators of the Marriage Matters Prayer Cards. Connect with them at www.knotproject.org.

Steve Ferguson is an Episcopal priest, retired Army officer, husband, father of three (one of whom wrote this book), and grandfather of seven. He lost his dear wife and best friend, Sandy, to pancreatic cancer in 2017. His passions are reading, motorcycle riding, and traveling, especially to visit his children and grandchildren. Steve lives in Tomball, Texas, with his chocolate lab, Annabelle, and he currently serves as Mission Integration/ Spiritual Care Coordinator for CHI St. Luke's Hospital at the Vintage in Houston, Texas.

Lauren Gaskill is an author and speaker and the founder of She Found Joy. Diagnosed with an incurable genetic disorder, Lauren is passionate about encouraging others to hold on to faith and learn how to find joy in every circumstance. She lives with her husband and beloved dog, Reese, just a few hours from the ocean in North Carolina. She can be found online at http://shefoundjoy.com.

Kathryn McDaniel is Catherine Bird's best gal pal and sister from another mister. One of her greatest passions has been helping others through her career, volunteer work, and personal life. She is currently focusing that passion on homeschooling her two sons and instilling in them the importance of serving others. She recently celebrated twenty years of marriage with her husband and fellow Aggie, Jody.

Bekah Pogue is an author, retreat leader, founder of Pasture, spiritual director-in-training, listener, writing and creative coach, and design enthusiast. She is most fully alive sitting on her porch listening to people share their hearts. She communicates from a space of intentionally climbing down the "someone" ladder in order that God—not she—is the one glorified. Bekah loves off-road wildflower picking, antiquing, dancing as she bakes, and exploring Nashville with her crew. She'd love to connect face-to-face, but until then, you can connect with her at www.bekahpogue.com.

Katie M. Reid is a devoted wife and busy mother of five loud, wonderful kids. She is the author of *Made like Martha: Good News for the Woman Who Gets Things Done*. Katie encourages women to find grace in the unraveling at www.katiemreid.com.

Bobbie Schae is the first to admit that she's a little bit of a hot mess who is just doing her best to honor him in the craziness of life. She hopes that by sharing her efforts to do so, she can shake a little salt and shine a little light and encourage you to do the same. Bobbie Schae is the founder of Build A Sister Up, where she is editor of the Build A Sister Up Collective. She is also a blogger, community builder, and encourager at www.bobbieschae.com.

Carey Scott. Word nerd. Storyteller. Life coach. Jesus girl. Raising two rock star kids. Author of the books *Untangled*, *Uncommon*, and *Unafraid*. Advocate for authenticity. Coffee lover. Pumpkin spice adorer. Deep water wader. Born Texan but Colorado dweller. Takes up space at www.careyscott.org.

Jodi Snider shares her chronic illness story on her blog www.overwhelmedwithgrace.com. She has also started a chronic illness support group called Buncha Sickies, where women encourage and lift each other up in their struggles. She has two softhearted children and an amazing husband who has been her constant earthly support.

Tracy Steel is a mentor, speaker, proud Air Force wife, and doting mommy of two spirited kiddos. She is also the author of *Images of His Beauty* and *A Redesigned Life*. You can read more of her ramblings about life and faith over at www.tracymsteel.com.

About the Illustrator

Shari Sasser is a graphic designer and illustrator motivated by the desire to use her God-given gifts and talents to serve God and his children while encouraging others to do the same. She currently serves as a Bible study leader for ladies and leads weekly music and devotions in local nursing homes. Previously, she served for many years as a Bible teacher and mentor for teenage girls. She and her husband are the proud parents of two young adults and currently reside in North Carolina. As a freelance artist, Shari creates illustrations and designs for a variety of clients. Her online portfolio is available to view at www.sharisasser.com.

About the Author

Catherine Bird is an author, speaker, Bible teacher, and sometimes a reluctant homeschooling mama, who also loves being a wife and a mom and often struggles to find balance between them all. She is genuine and not without a sense of humor about her walk with Jesus, which includes plenty of bumps, stumbles, and falls. We serve a good and faithful God who asks for our love in return. Catherine is passionate about encouraging others to embrace this truth. To that end, throughout her ministry, she has worked with women, teens, and tweens to encourage, empower, and equip each in their own journey of faith.

Catherine is the author of *Becoming a Girl of Grace: A Joint Bible Study for Tween Girls and Their Moms*, *Building Circles of Grace*, and *Preparing a Way: An Advent Devotional for Tween Girls and Their Moms* (available for free download at www.catherinebird.net).

Catherine and her family currently live near Austin, Texas. When she is not at her desk writing, Catherine can often be found in yoga class, scoping out some fun new hiking destination with her family, or curled up in a comfy chair on her patio with her colored pencils. She also believes wholeheartedly in laughing until your belly hurts, Taco Tuesday, and Texas Aggie football. Life is sweeter with community, and friends are always welcome to pop by Catherine's online home at www.catherinebird.net.